Lonely Planet

POCKET

PRAGUE

TOP EXPERIENCES · LOCAL LIFE

Y0-BQT-167

MARC DI DUCA,
MARK BAKER, BARBARA WOOLSEY

Contents

Plan Your Trip 4

Charles Bridge (p80)
PYTY/SHUTTERSTOCK©

Explore Prague   29

Survival Guide   145

Special Features

COVID-19

We have re-checked every business in this book before publication to ensure that it is still open after the COVID-19 outbreak. However, the economic and social impacts of COVID-19 will continue to be felt long after the outbreak has been contained, and many businesses, services and events referenced in this guide may experience ongoing restrictions. Some businesses may be temporarily closed, have changed their opening hours and services, or require bookings; some unfortunately could have closed permanently. We suggest you check with venues before visiting for the latest information.

Prague's Top Experiences

Explore Prague Castle (p32)

Marvel at St Vitus Cathedral (p38)

Gather in the Old Town Square (p78)

LUCIANO MORTULA - LGM/SHUTTERSTOCK©

TTSTUDIO/SHUTTERSTOCK©

Walk Across Iconic Charles Bridge (p80)

Wander the Old Jewish Cemetery (p66)

MARIA CHAPA HAMMEKEN/SHUTTERSTOCK ©

ALESSANDRO0770/SHUTTERSTOCK©

Gain Insight at the Jewish Museum (p64)

Get Your Art Fix at Veletržní Palác (p136)

TICHR SHUTTERSTOCK

DIETMAR RAUSCHER/SHUTTERSTOCK ©

DŮM MÓDY

Stroll along Buzzing Wenceslas Square (p98)

Hike up Petřín Hill (p48)

DAVID IONUT/SHUTTERSTOCK ©

ISOGOOD_PATRICK/SHUTTERSTOCK ©

Admire the Baroque Beauty of Loreta (p40)

Dining Out

The restaurant scene in Prague gets better with each passing year. Recent years have seen an explosion in vegetarian and vegan restaurants, though meat is bigger than ever, both in traditional Czech restaurants and in hipster burger eateries.

Czech Cuisine

Czech food in Prague can be hit-and-miss. Traditional dishes such as roast pork and sliced bread dumplings (*vepřová pečeně s knedlíky*) or roast beef in cream sauce (*svíčková na smetaně*) can be bland (as at many touristy restaurants) or memorable (when prepared by someone who cares) – choose your restaurants carefully. Other, often delicious, Czech staples include pork knuckle (*vepřové koleno*), duck (*kachna*) and goulash (*guláš*; pictured above), served with either beef or pork and bread dumplings.

International Foods

International food trends come and go with the same regularity as in other large cities. Alongside standard international cuisines such as French and Italian – and especially pizza – Czechs have developed a taste for good Indian and Asian cooking as well as for steakhouses and Mexican food. The latest trends include steakhouses, burgers and artisan food.

Vegetarian Options

The last decade or so has witnessed a revolution in healthy dining, with a growing number of vegetarian and vegan restaurants sprouting up around town. Alas, vegetarian options at traditional Czech restaurants seem to be as limited as ever, with the best bet being the ubiquitous (but often excellent) fried cheese (*smažený sýr*), served with a dollop of cranberry and/or tartar sauce.

STEPANEK PHOTOGRAPHY/SHUTTERSTOCK©

Best Fine Dining

Field Michelin-starred dining in the Old Town. (p72)

Augustine Relaxed sophistication combined with the restaurant's own beer. (p56)

Best Czech Cuisine

U Modré Kachničky Beautiful, classy restaurant in Malá Strana where the speciality is duck in many guises. (p57)

The Eatery Sophisticated Holešovice restaurant serving modern takes on Czech classics. (p140)

Vinohradský Parlament A 21st-century take on the Czech pub. (p130)

Best for Vegetarians

Vegan's Prague Completely plant-based restaurant on the main tourist route through Malá Strana. (p58)

Lehká Hlava Exotic dining room with an emphasis on fresh preparation. (p90)

Best for a Quick Lunch

Mistral Café Possibly the coolest bistro in the Old Town. (p72)

Havelská Koruna Self-service canteen serving cheap, institutional Czech food. (p91)

Hostinec U Tunelu Quality lunch menu at this atmospheric tavern. (p130)

Prices & Tipping

○ Some places charge a small *couvert* (to cover bread and condiments); this should be clearly marked on the menu.

○ If service and food were good, round up the bill to the nearest 50Kč or 100Kč as a tip.

Bar Open

Drinking is the Czechs' national pastime, so it's no surprise that Prague is an imbiber's playground. On practically every corner, there's a pub, wine bar, beer hall or cocktail lounge. Despite passing interest in wine and cocktails over the years, Prague remains a beer city, with the national brands now joined by quality microbrew beers.

Beer Basics

When it comes to beer (*pivo*), Czechs prefer light lagers (*světlé*) to darker beers (*tmavé*), though most pubs serve both. Pilsner Urquell is considered the best Czech brand, though Gambrinus, Budvar and Prague's own Staropramen are popular. Czech beers are usually labelled either *dvanáctka* (12°) or *desítka* (10°), but this doesn't refer to alcohol content (most beers are 4.5% to 5%). The 12° beers tend to be heavier and stronger than 10° beers.

Microbrews & 'Tank' Beer

The global craft-beer trend has reached the Czech Republic and is most pronounced in Prague, which boasts around a dozen brew pubs where DIY brewers proffer their own concoctions, usually accompanied by good traditional Czech cooking. To compete with the microbrews, the larger breweries have come up with several innovations, including offering unfiltered (*nefiltrované*) beer and hauling beer directly to pubs in supersized tanks

(called, unsurprisingly, *tankové pivo*). Obscure beers from around the Czech Republic are also well worth trying.

Best for Beer

Prague Beer Museum Not a museum but a hugely popular pub, with 30 varieties on tap. (p125)

Klášterní Pivovar Strahov Excellent microbrew beer at the Strahov Monastery. (p45)

U Zlatého Tygra The classic Prague drinking den, where Václav Havel took Bill Clinton in 1994 to show him a real Czech pub. (p91)

Pivovarský Dům Popular microbrewery with several

ARIEH/SHUTTERSTOCK©

beers on tap and decent Czech food. (p117)

Letná Beer Garden A big beer garden with stunning views over Prague. (p141)

U Tří růží Tradition-reviving brewpub cooking up six different types of lager. (p93)

Best Cocktail Bars

Hemingway Bar Snug and sophisticated hideaway. (p93)

Tretter's New York Bar Upmarket New York–style cocktail bar. (p74)

Best for Wine

Le Caveau Cosy Vinohrady watering hole and deli features excellent French wine. (p125)

Café Kaaba Retro cafe that stocks wines from around the world and sells by the glass. (p132)

Best Cafes

Grand Cafe Orient A stunning cubist gem with a sunny balcony. (p93)

Cafe Louvre Prague's most agreeable grand cafe and billiards hall. (p116)

Kavárna Obecní dům A legendary Viennese-style coffee house inside an art-nouveau landmark. (p93)

Café Savoy This gorgeous coffee house does a lavish breakfast. (p56)

Kavárna Slavia Prague's most famous cafe opposite the National Theatre. (p116)

Good to Know

○ Pub tabs are usually recorded on a slip of paper on your table; don't write on it or lose it.

○ To pay up and go, say *zaplatím* (I'll pay).

Treasure Hunt

Though the streets are lined with stores, Prague doesn't initially seem a particularly inspiring shopping city. But if you know where to look, you can find above-average versions of classic souvenirs: Bohemian crystal and glassware, garnet and puppets. Farm-produced beauty products and old-school children's toys also make great gifts.

RICHARD NEBESKY/LONELY PLANET©

For mainstream shopping, central Na Příkopě boasts international chains from H&M to Zara. For the most part, you can put your wallet away along Wenceslas Square (also a good way to avoid pickpocketing). Instead, explore the Old Town's winding alleyways. Ritzy Pařížská is often called Prague's Champs Élysées and is lined with luxury brands such as Cartier, Hugo Boss and Ferragamo. Dlouhá, Dušní and surrounding streets house some original fashion boutiques, while even central Celetná contains a worthwhile stop or two.

Best for Unique Souvenirs

Botanicus Rustic-chic beauty products from this popular old apothecary. (p95)

Manufaktura Specialises in traditional crafts and wooden toys. (pictured above; p95)

Bric A Brac Aladdin's cave of Prague junk and yester-year jumble. (p95)

Best for Design & Glass

Modernista Czech cubist and art-deco design with cool ceramics, jewellery, posters and books. (p95)

Moser Ornate Bohemian glass objects. (p109)

Artěl Traditional glass-making meets stylish modern design. (p59)

Best for Books & Toys

Marionety Truhlář Quirky shop stocks traditional marionettes from workshops around Czechia. (p59)

Shakespeare & Sons More than just a bookshop – a literary hang-out. (p59)

Kavka Coffee-table art books you won't find anywhere else. (p94)

Best for Fashion

Klára Nademlýnská Boutique belonging to one of Czechia's top fashion designers. (p75)

Baťa Shoes from one of the country's most illustrious brands. (p109)

Under the Radar

KRISTYNA HENKEOVA/SHUTTERSTOCK ©

Post-Covid, many things are bound to fall into place in a different way than they were before the pandemic struck. Here are a few tips on what you might want to do differently during your visit and what might be cool when the tourists finally return.

Book Direct

One of the symbols of Prague's pre-pandemic overtourism image was Airbnb, a brand that's taken a battering in the past few years, having been threatened with regulation, lobbied against by angry local residents, decimated by Covid and declared a taxable business in 2021 by the Czech courts. Consider avoiding the slightly toxic karma around the city's short-term rental market by booking direct with hotels, guesthouses and hosts.

Sustainable Fashion

See that queue snaking down Wenceslas Square? A line for classical music tickets or a packed out beer hall? Well, no, it's the daily ordeal to get into Primark, the bargain clothes chain. Why not call a halt to throwaway fashion by giving your custom to Prague's local designers, charity shops and vintage clothing emporia, instead?

Free Tours

'Free tours' are bound to make a post-Covid comeback, foreign guides leading groups of foreigners a merry dance through the old centre, a hefty tip expected at the end. But there are plenty of other tour companies who dig deeper for a more authentic and accurate experience.

Cool Karlín

It's difficult to tell where the dice will fall in coming years as far as Prague's coolest up-and-coming neighbourhood (pictured) is concerned. But we'd bet it will still be Karlín, the hottest area most tourists never visit.

Art

The city's art holdings were pilfered over the centuries by various invaders, and museums here lack the depth of galleries in Vienna and Paris. That said, the National Gallery's collections are strong in medieval art, baroque and early-20th-century art, when Czech artists came into their own.

SCULPTURE: PROUDY BY DAVID ČERNÝ;
DOUG MCKINLAY/LONELY PLANET©

Best Art Museums

Veletržní Palác National Gallery's jaw-dropping collection of art from the 20th and 21st centuries. (p136)

Šternberg Palace National Gallery's collection of European art includes works by Goya and Rembrandt. (p43)

Mucha Museum Sensuous art-nouveau posters, paintings and decorative panels by Alfons Mucha. (p103)

Convent of St Agnes Collection of medieval and early Renaissance art is a treasure house of glowing Gothic altar paintings. (p70)

Best Public Art

K Kafka's rotating, peeling head is now Prague's most prominent piece of public art; by David Černý. (p114)

Miminka Ten creepy babies crawling atop the Žižkov TV Tower, by David Černý. (p129)

Proudy David Černý sculpture features two guys peeing into a puddle shaped like Czechia. (pictured above; p51)

Franz Kafka Monument This unusual sculpture has a mini-Franz sitting piggyback on his own headless body. (p71)

Museums

TOMAS PILLER/500PX©

Prague has tonnes of museums scattered around the city. Most museums cater to specific interests, but alas, many of the collections are of the old-school variety: static objects displayed behind thick glass. The recently refurbished, interactive and loads-of-fun National Technical Museum is a welcome exception and great for kids.

Prague Jewish Museum Displays the development of centuries of Jewish life and traditions with exhibitions in around half a dozen surviving synagogues. The highlight of the experience is to walk through the evocative former Jewish cemetery, with its thousands of jagged-edged tombstones. (p64)

National Technical Museum The Czech Republic's industrial heritage is on riotous display, with interactive exhibits and giant locomotives. (pictured above; p139)

National Museum Recently reopened after years of renovation. (p103)

Prague City Museum Get the low-down on Prague's history at this superb museum. (p113)

Museum of Decorative Arts A feast for the eyes, full of 16th- to 19th-century artefacts, such as furniture, tapestries, porcelain and glass. (p69)

Lobkowicz Palace Discover paintings by Cranach and Canaletto, original musical scores annotated by Mozart and Beethoven, and an impressive collection of musical instruments. (p36)

Discounted Entry

o Most museums offer discounted family tickets.

o The **Prague Card** (www.praguecard.com) offers free or discounted entry to around 50 sights, including many museums.

For Kids

Czechs are very family-oriented, so there are plenty of activities for children around the city. An increasing number of Prague restaurants cater specifically for children, with play areas and so on, and many offer a children's menu – even if they don't, they can usually provide smaller portions for a lower price.

ALEXEY PYSHNENKO/500PX©

Into the Fresh Air

A great outing for kids (and parents) is Prague Zoo, located north of the centre in Troja. In addition, there are several other patches of green around town, such as Stromovka, where you can spread a blanket and let the kids run free. Petřín is a beautiful park on a hill where parents and kids alike can take a break from sightseeing, and climb the Petřín Lookout Tower for terrific views over Prague.

Best of the Outdoors

Stromovka Prague's largest central park, with lots of playgrounds. (p140)

Prague Zoo Aside from the animals, attractions include a miniature cable car. (pictured above; p139)

Petřín Funicular Kids will get a thrill riding this funicular to the top of the hill. (p49)

Best Indoor Activities

National Technical Museum A must-stop for inquisitive adolescents and techie parents. (p139)

Miniature Museum Kids will love the titchy exhibits at this quirky museum. (p43)

Apple Museum Tech-crazed tots and teens will adore this temple to all things Jobs. (p86)

Half-Price Tickets

○ Kids up to age 15 normally pay half-price for attractions (under six years free).

○ On public transport, kids aged from six to 15 years pay half-price.

For Free

Once famously inexpensive, Prague is no longer cheap – there's little on offer without a price attached. That said, in a city this beautiful, you don't need to spend lots of time (or money) on pricey museums. The parks and gardens, including the hilltop vista from Letná Gardens, are free, as is the street entertainment on Charles Bridge.

COURTYARDPIX/SHUTTERSTOCK ©

Prague Castle Without a Ticket

Admission to the interiors of Prague Castle, including St Vitus Cathedral, costs a bit. But many people don't realize that the castle grounds, including the surrounding gardens, are free to roam at your leisure. The highlights of a visit are the views over Malá Strana and the hourly changing of the guard; the grandest show is performed daily at noon.

Best Free Sights

Nový Svět Quarter A delightful alternative to Prague Castle's Golden Lane. (p44)

Petřín Hill Entrance to the park is gratis; skip the funicular and just hike up. (p48)

Astronomical Clock The hourly chiming is public and free. (p79)

Vyšehrad Cemetery This beautiful cemetery is the final resting place for composers Smetana and Dvořák, as well as art-nouveau artist Alfons Mucha. (p121)

Letná Gardens The sweeping views are free; drinks from the beer garden cost extra. (p139)

More for Free

○ Ask at tourist information offices about free concerts, theatrical performances and cultural events happening during your visit.

○ Visits to most churches (except St Vitus Cathedral and St Nicholas Church) are free.

Architecture

Prague is an open-air museum of architecture; most of the centre enjoys UNESCO protection. Its architectural heritage was built up over the centuries, with the earliest Romanesque buildings dating back nearly 1000 years. Later, Renaissance, baroque, neoclassical and art-nouveau styles were added as fashions changed.

DOUG MCKINLAY/LONELY PLANET©

Best Romanesque & Gothic

Rotunda of St Martin Tiny, circular church in Vyšehrad is reputedly Prague's oldest standing building and a perfect example of Romanesque architecture. (p121)

St Vitus Cathedral Gothic to the tips of its famous spires. (p38)

Charles Bridge Prague's most famous bridge is a Gothic landmark. (p80)

Best Renaissance & Baroque

St Nicholas Church In Malá Strana, the mother of all baroque churches in Prague. (p53)

Loreta This pilgrimage site is modelled after the Italian original. (p40)

Best National Revival & Art Nouveau

Municipal House Glittering art nouveau. (p85)

Grand Hotel Evropa Fading grandeur at this ornate art-nouveau hotel and cafe. (p99)

Best Modern Architecture

Church of the Most Sacred Heart of Our Lord Prague's most unusual church by Slovene architect, Jože Plečnik. (pictured above; p129)

Veletržní Palác This mammoth functionalist structure doesn't look like your everyday palace. (p136)

Delve Deeper

○ For more on Prague architecture, take a tour with Prague Unknown (www.praha neznama.cz).

○ *Prague: An Architectural Guide* is a photographic encyclopaedia by Smith, Schonberg and Sedlakova.

History

Prague history reads like a novel, chock-full of characters riding the city's fortunes from the heights of the Holy Roman Empire to the depths of the Eastern bloc (with chills and spills between). Fortunately, the city was spared mass destruction in WWII, and every building, from the castle to the corner shop, has a story.

CRISTIAN PUSCASU/SHUTTERSTOCK ©

Best Royal Sights

Vyšehrad Citadel Where it all began – Prague's oldest fortification. (p120)

Prague Castle Seat of Czech power for 1000 years. (p32)

Astronomical Clock Ancient mechanical marvel that still chimes on the hour. (p79)

St Nicholas Church The height of Habsburg-inspired baroque splendour. (p53)

Best National Revival

Municipal House Art-nouveau apogee of art and national aspiration. (p85)

National Theatre Built to showcase emerging Czech music and drama. (p118)

Best for Modern History

National Memorial to the Heroes of the Heydrich Terror Site where seven

Czechoslovak partisans took refuge from the Nazis – and met tragic ends – in 1942. (pictured above; p114)

TV Tower Communist power at its most potent. (p129)

John Lennon Wall This graffiti-splattered memorial was repainted each time the secret police whitewashed over it. (p51)

Four Perfect Days

Day 1

ARTONO/SHUTTERSTOCK©

Day 2

MACIEJ BLEDOWSKI/SHUTTERSTOCK©

Just one day in Prague? Focus on major sights. Start early, joining the crowd below the **Astronomical Clock** (p79) for the hourly chiming, then wander through the **Old Town Square** (p78), taking in the spectacular array of architectural styles and the spires of the **Church of Our Lady Before Týn** (p79). From there, amble through the winding alleys of the Old Town on your way to one of Prague's most famous landmarks, **Charles Bridge** (p80). Stop for lunch at **Cukrkávalimonáda** (p57) before hiking up to **Prague Castle** (p32) through Malá Strana. Visiting the castle and **St Vitus Cathedral** (pictured; p38) will take the rest of the day. For dinner, treat yourself to a meal with a view at **Villa Richter** (p44) nearby.

Spend the morning exploring the quaint backstreets and Kampa gardens of Malá Strana, one of the city's oldest districts. Catch the **Petřín Funicular** (p49) to enjoy sweeping views from the **Lookout Tower** (p49) at the top of Petřín Hill. From here, find the serene path that crosses over to the **Strahov Monastery** (pictured; p43), and then head downhill along Nerudova. Treat yourself to a late lunch at the riverside **Hergetova Cihelná** (p58).

Cross the river in the afternoon to check out the **Jewish Museum** (p64). Later stop by the box office of the **National Theatre** (p118) to see if any last-minute tickets are available to the opera or ballet. Before the show, have a light meal at **Cafe Louvre** (p116).

Day 3

VERONIKA PRIMM/LONELY PLANET©

Start with coffee at the famous **Kavárna Slavia** (pictured; p116), choosing a table looking across the river to Prague Castle. From here, walk up Národní třída to **Wenceslas Square** (p98), taking time to see the nearby sights, including the **National Museum** (p103) and **St Wenceslas Statue** (p99). Plan lunch at **Výtopna** (p105).

From here it's an easy metro trip to **Vyšehrad** (p120), where you can wander the ruins and visit the graves of Dvořak and Mucha in the cemetery, as well as admiring the river views.

Spend the evening in Vinohrady or Žižkov, choosing one of the area's excellent restaurants, such as **Vinohradský Parlament** (p130) or **The Tavern** (p131).

Day 4

DALIU/SHUTTERSTOCK©

It's time to see a different part of Prague. Start on Old Town Square and walk down elegant Pařížská, before crossing the river and climbing to **Letná Gardens** (pictured; p139). Admire the views from the top, then make your way east to **Letná Beer Garden** (p141) for an early lunch.

Suitably fortified, it's a short walk to the **National Technical Museum** (p139) – perfect if you've got kids. If you've still got the energy, visit Prague's best (and most underrated) art museum, **Veletržní Palác** (p136), before taking the tram back towards town. Enjoy a meal on the rooftop terrace at **U Prince** (p85) to lift a glass to this lovely city on your last night in Prague.

Need to Know

For detailed information, see Survival Guide (p145)

Currency
Czech crown
(Koruna česká; Kč)

Language
Czech

Visas
Generally not required
for stays of up to three
months.

Money
ATMs widely available
and credit cards are
accepted at many
restaurants and hotels.

Mobile Phones
Czechia uses GSM 900,
compatible with mobile
phones from the rest of
Europe, Australia and
New Zealand (but not
most North American
phones).

Time
Central European Time
(GMT plus one hour)

Tipping
Standard practice
in pubs, cafes and
restaurants is to round
up the bill to the nearest
50Kč or 100Kč if service
has been good.

Daily Budget

Budget: Less than €80
Dorm beds: €10–20
Cheap supermarkets for self-catering
Admission to major tourist attractions: €10

Midrange: €80–200
Double room: €120–200
Three-course dinner in casual restaurant: €30

Top end: More than €200
Double room or suite at luxury hotel: €200–260
Seven-course tasting menu in top restaurant: €120

Useful Websites

Lonely Planet (www.lonelyplanet.com/czech-republic/
prague) Destination info, hotel bookings, traveller forum
and more.

Prague City Tourism (www.prague.eu) Prague's official
tourism portal.

Prague.com (www.prague.com) A city guide and booking
website.

Prague Public Transit (www.dpp.cz) Handy journey
planner for all public transport.

Arriving in Prague

Public transport and taxis easily available from both arrival hubs.

✈ Václav Havel Airport Prague

Around 15km by road from the Old Town Square.

Taxis Wait outside the terminals. 700Kč.

Bus 119 runs regularly to Nádraží Veleslavín metro station. 32Kč. The Airport Express (AE) bus runs every 30 minutes direct to Hlavní Nádraží train station. 60Kč.

🚆 Praha Hlavní Nádraží Train Station

The main train station is situated in Nové Město, near Wenceslas Square.

Metro The station is on red line C, with connections to Holešovice and Vyšehrad. Change at Můstek or Florenc for other destinations.

Walk The city centre is within walking distance.

Getting Around

Prague's public-transport system is one of Europe's best. Most visitors will get everywhere they need to on foot, metro or tram.

Ⓜ Metro

Prague's metro system (pictured) runs from 5am to midnight, with fast, frequent services.

🚋 Tram

Travelling on trams is a quintessentially Prague experience. Regular trams run from 5am to midnight. After midnight, night trams (91 to 99) rumble across the city about every 40 minutes.

🚕 Taxi

Taxis are convenient when you're in a hurry, but be careful of scams. Look for the 'Taxi Fair Place' stations in key tourist areas.

MARTYN JANDULA/SHUTTERSTOCK ©

Prague Neighbourhoods

Prague Castle & Hradĉany (p31)
This refined hilltop district is defined by the castle complex that gives Prague its dreamy, fairy-tale-like appearance.

Old Town Square & Staré Město (p77)
Gothic spires, art-nouveau architecture, a quirky astronomical clock and horse-drawn carriages crowd this colourful, famous old square.

Old Jewish Cemetery

Jewish Museum

Prague Castle

St Vitus Cathedral ◉ ◉

Loreta ◉

◉ ◉

Charles ◉ Old Town Square & Astronomical Clock
Bridge

Petřín Hill ◉

Malá Strana & Petřín Hill (p47)
Quaint, cobblestoned streets, red roofs, ancient cloisters and a peaceful hillside park characterise Prague's charming 'Lesser Quarter'.

Nové Město (p111)
Cool modern architecture and quiet riverside cafes are the crowning glories of this underrated neighbourhood.

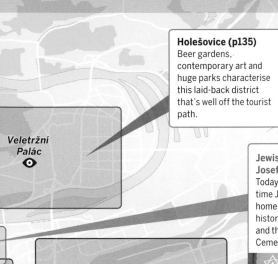

Holešovice (p135)
Beer gardens, contemporary art and huge parks characterise this laid-back district that's well off the tourist path.

Veletržní Palác 👁

Jewish Museum & Josefov (p63)
Today, Prague's one-time Jewish ghetto is home to a cluster of historic synagogues and the eerie Old Jewish Cemetery.

👁 *Wenceslas Square*

Wenceslas Square & Around (p97)
Once a horse market, this huge square has been the site of many important moments in Czech history.

Vinohrady & Žižkov (p123)
The locals' residential neighbourhood of choice, this leafy area contains many of Prague's hippest bars and cafes.

Explore
Prague

Prague tram ONDREJ_NOVOTNY_92/SHUTTERSTOCK©

Explore ◉

Prague Castle & Hradčany

St Vitus Cathedral, rising from the heart of Prague Castle, is rarely out of view when you're wandering around Prague. The promontory on which the castle sits is called Hradčany, an area packed with fascinating sites, both religious and secular.

The Short List

○ **Prague Castle (p32)** *Prague's magnificent Old Royal Palace that documents the history of Czechia's most famous historical complex.*

○ **St Vitus Cathedral (p38)** *The Czechs' top temple is built in a hotchpotch of architectural styles and packed with artistic treasures.*

○ **Loreta (p40)** *One of the most significant places of pilgrimage, with the Santa Casa at its heart.*

○ **Strahov Library (p43)** *The country's largest and most ornate monastery library.*

○ **Golden Lane (p34)** *Street of miniature cottages at the castle, where Franz Kafka once stayed and wrote.*

Getting There & Around

🚋 Take 22 to Pražský hrad then walk five minutes, or to Pohořelec and then walk downhill.

Ⓜ Take Line A to Malostranská, then climb the steps.

Neighbourhood Map on p42

Prague Castle and St Vitus Cathedral SVETJEKOLEM/SHUTTERSTOCK©

Top Experience 📷
Explore Prague Castle

Known simply as hrad (castle) to locals, Prague Castle was founded by 9th-century Přemysl princes and grew haphazardly as subsequent rulers built additions. Today, it's a humungous complex with three large courtyards. Many Czech rulers have resided here; one notable exception is the first post-communist president, Václav Havel: in 1989, he plumped for the comforts of his own home instead.

◎ MAP P42, E2

www.hrad.cz

Hradčanské náměstí 1

adult from 250Kč

🕑 gardens 10am-6pm Apr-Oct, historic buildings 9am-5pm Apr-Oct, to 4pm Nov-Mar

Ⓜ Malostranská, 🚊 22, 23

Castle Entrance

The castle's main gate, on Hradčany Square, is flanked by huge, 18th-century statues of battling Titans that dwarf the castle guards below. Playwright-turned-president Václav Havel hired the Czech costume designer on the film *Amadeus* to redesign the guards' uniforms and instigated a changing-of-the-guard ceremony – the most impressive display is at noon.

Prague Castle Picture Gallery

In 1648 an invading Swedish army looted Emperor Rudolf II's art collection (as well as making off with the original bronze statues in the Wallenstein Garden). The **gallery** (adult/child 100/50Kč, admission incl with Prague Castle Tour C ticket; ◷9am-5pm Apr-Oct, to 4pm Nov-Mar) in these converted Renaissance stables displays what was left, as well as replacement works, including some by Rubens, Tintoretto and Titian.

Plečnik Monolith

In the third courtyard, a noteworthy feature near St Vitus Cathedral is a huge granite monolith dedicated to the victims of WWI, designed by Slovene architect Jože Plečnik in 1928. Nearby is a copy of the castle's famous statue of St George slaying the dragon.

Old Royal Palace

The palace's highlight is the high-Gothic vaulted roof of Vladislav Hall (Vladislavský sál; 1493–1502), beneath which all the presidents of the Czech Republic have been sworn in. There's also a balcony off the hall with great city views and a door to the former Bohemian Chancellery, where the Second Defenestration of Prague occurred in 1618.

★ Top Tips

o The castle buildings open at 9am; be there a few minutes early to beat the crowds.

o You'll need at least half a day to explore the castle grounds.

o Guided tours of the castle in English can be arranged in advance by calling 🗐 224 373 584. Tours last around an hour and leave from the information centres.

o To catch music and cultural events at the castle grounds, check out www .kulturanahrade. cz for a schedule of events.

✕ Take a Break

There are several places scattered around the castle grounds to stop for a coffee or cold drink. Our favourite – also good for lunch – is the lovely **Lobkowicz Palace Café** (p44), located on the ground level of Lobkowicz Palace.

Story of Prague Castle

One of the castle's most compelling **exhibitions** (adult/child 140/70Kč; 🕑9am-5pm, to 4pm Nov-Mar), with an outstanding collection of armour, jewellery, glassware, furniture and other artefacts from more than 1000 years of the castle's history. A particularly memorable sight is the skeleton of the pre-Christian 'warrior', still encased in the earth where archaeologists found him within the castle grounds.

Basilica of St George

Behind a brick-red facade lies the Czechs' best-preserved Romanesque **church** (Bazilika sv Jiří; www.hrad.cz; Jiřské náměstí; admission included with Prague Castle tour A & B tickets; 🕑9am-5pm Apr-Oct, to 4pm Nov-Mar). The original was established in the 10th century by Vratislav I (the father of St Wenceslas), who is still buried here, as is St Ludmilla. It's also popular for small concert performances.

Golden Lane

The tiny, colourful cottages along this cobbled **alley** (Zlatá ulička; admission incl with Prague Castle tour A & B tickets; 🕑9am-5pm Apr-Oct, to 4pm Nov-Mar) were built in the 16th century for the castle guard's sharpshooters, but were later used by goldsmiths, squatters and artists, including writer Franz Kafka, who stayed at his sister's house at No 22 from 1916 to 1917.

Golden Lane MO WU/SHUTTERSTOCK ©

Kings & Castles

Prague's history, filled with royal betrayals, people tossing each other out of windows, and one man famously being burnt at the stake, makes *The Tudors* look tame by comparison.

In the Beginning

The name 'Bohemia', still used to describe Czechia's western half, comes from a Celtic tribe, the Boii, who lived here for centuries before Slavic tribes arrived around the 6th century. The 9th-century Přemysl dynasty built the earliest section of today's Prague Castle in the 9th century, and also included one Václav, or Wenceslas, of 'Good King' Christmas-carol fame.

The Good Times

After the Přemysl dynasty died out, Prague came under the control of the family that eventually produced Holy Roman Emperor Charles IV (1316–78). Under his rule, the city blossomed. Charles, whose mother was Czech, elevated Prague's official status and went on a construction spree, building the New Town (Nové Město) and Charles Bridge, founding Charles University and adding St Vitus Cathedral to the castle.

University rector Jan Hus led the 15th-century Hussite movement, which challenged what many saw as the corrupt practices of the Catholic Church. Hus was burned at the stake at Constance in 1415 for 'heresy' – this kicked off decades of sectarian fighting.

Habsburg Rule

In 1526 the Czech lands came under the rule of the Austrian Habsburgs. With the Reformation in full swing in Europe, tensions between the Catholic Habsburgs and reformist Czechs inevitably surfaced. In 1618 Bohemian rebels threw two Catholic councillors from a Prague Castle window, sparking the Thirty Years' War (1618–48). Following the defeat of the Czech nobility in 1620 at the Battle of White Mountain (Bílá Hora), Czechs lost their independence to Austria for 300 years.

Rosenberg Palace

Originally built as the grand residence of the Rosenberg family, this 16th-century Renaissance-style **palace** (Rožmberský palác; Jiřská 1; admission incl with Prague Castle tour A ticket; ⊙9am-5pm Apr-Oct, to 4pm Nov-Mar) was later repurposed by Empress Maria Theresa as a 'Residence for Noblewomen' to house 30 unmarried women at a time. Today, one section of the palace re-creates the style of an 18th-century noblewoman's apartment using artefacts from the Prague Castle's depository.

Lobkowicz Palace

The 16th-century **Lobkowicz Palace** (Lobkovický palác; 📞 233 312 925; www.lobkowicz.com; Jiřská 3; adult/concession 295/220Kč; 🕐10am-6pm) houses a private museum known as the Princely Collections, with priceless paintings, furniture and musical memorabilia. An included audio guide dictated by owner William Lobkowicz and his family brings the displays to life, making this one of the castle's most interesting attractions.

Royal Garden

Powder Bridge (Prašný most; 1540) spans the Stag Moat (Jelení příkop) en route to the spacious Renaissance-style **Royal Garden** (Královská zahrada; admission free; 🕐10am-6pm Apr-Oct), dating from 1534. The most beautiful building is the Ball-Game House (Míčovna; 1569), a masterpiece of Renaissance sgraffito where the Habsburgs once played badminton. East is the Summer Palace (Letohrádek; 1538–60) and west the former Riding School (Jízdárna; 1695).

Southern Gardens

The three gardens lined up below the castle's southern wall – **Paradise Garden**, the **Hartig Garden** and the **Garden on the Ramparts** – offer superb views over Malá Strana's rooftops. Enter from the west via the New Castle Steps or from the east via the Old Castle Steps.

Visiting Prague Castle

There are three kinds of tickets for Prague Castle (each valid for two days), which allow entry to different combinations of sights:

Tour A (adult/child/family 350/175/700Kč) Includes St Vitus Cathedral, Old Royal Palace, Story of Prague Castle, Basilica of St George, Powder Tower, Golden Lane, Daliborka and Rosenberg Palace.

Tour B (adult/child/family 250/125/500Kč) Includes St Vitus Cathedral, Old Royal Palace, Basilica of St George, Golden Lane and Daliborka.

Tour C (adult/child/family 350/175/700Kč) Includes St Vitus Treasury and Prague Castle Picture Gallery.

You can buy tickets at either of two information centres in the **Second** (📞 224 372 423; 🕐9am-5pm Apr-Oct, to 4pm Nov-Mar) and **Third Courtyards** (📞 224 372 434; 🕐9am-5pm Apr-Oct, to 4pm Nov-Mar), or from ticket offices at the entrances to some of the individual sights.

Prague Castle

Old Castle Steps

Lobkowicz Palace Café

Lobkowicz Palace

Rosenberg Palace

Golden Lane

Stag Moat

Basilica of St George

Royal Garden

St George's Square

Story of Prague Castle

Old Royal Palace

Southern Gardens

Third Courtyard

St Vitus Cathedral

Plečník Monolith

Powder Bridge

Information Centre

New Castle Steps

Second Courtyard

Prague Castle Picture Gallery

Information Centre

First Courtyard

Castle Entrance

Hradčany Sq

Top Experience 📷
Marvel at St Vitus Cathedral

Czechia's most noteworthy church was begun in 1344. Though at first it appears Gothic, much of St Vitus Cathedral was only completed in time for its belated consecration in 1929. The coronations of Bohemia's kings were held here until the mid-19th century. Today it's the seat of Prague's Archbishop and the final resting place of some of the nation's most illustrious figures – kings, princes, even saints.

👁 MAP P42, E2

Katedrála sv Víta

📞 257 531 622

www.katedralasvate
hovita.cz

🕐 9am-5pm Mon-Sat
Apr-Oct, from noon Sun, to
4pm Nov-Mar

🚊 22, 23

Stained-Glass Windows

The interior is flooded with colour from stained-glass windows created by eminent Czech artists of the early 20th century. In the third chapel on the northern side (to the left as you enter) is one by art-nouveau artist Alfons Mucha, depicting the lives of Sts Cyril and Methodius.

Golden Gate

The cathedral's south entrance is known as the Golden Gate (Zlatá brána), an elegant, triple-arched Gothic porch designed by Peter Parler.

Royal Oratory

Kings addressed their subjects from the grand, intricately crafted oratory (1493), which appears to be woven with gnarled tree branches. This striking centrepiece exemplifies late-Gothic aesthetics.

Tomb of St John of Nepomuk

Nepomuk was a priest and a religious martyr; it's said that hundreds of years after his death, when his body was exhumed, his tongue was found 'still alive'. The Church canonised him and commissioned this elaborate silver sarcophagus for his reburial. (Scientists later showed that the 'tongue' was actually brain tissue congealed in blood.)

Chapel of St Wenceslas

This is the most beautiful of the cathedral's side chapels, with walls adorned with gilded panels containing polished slabs of semiprecious stones. Murals from the early 16th century depict scenes from the life of the Czechs' patron saint, while even older frescoes show scenes from the life of Jesus. On the southern side, a small door – locked with seven locks – leads to the coronation chamber, where the Bohemian crown jewels are kept.

★ Top Tips

o Try to arrive first thing in the morning, when the crowds are smaller.

o Entry to the cathedral is included in both A and B Prague Castle combined-entry tickets.

o For spectacular views, climb the stairway to the cathedral's tower.

✗ Take a Break

Before braving the crowds, fortify with a steaming cup of jasmine tea or a light meal at **Malý Buddha** (p44), located outside the castle complex a short walk from the main entrance.

Top Experience 📷

Admire the Baroque Beauty of Loreta

The Loreta is a baroque pilgrimage site financed by the noble Lobkowicz family in 1626. It was designed as a replica of the Santa Casa (the home of the Virgin Mary) in the Holy Land. Legend has it that the original was carried by angels to the Italian town of Loreto as the Turks were advancing on Nazareth. The Loreta's original counter-reformation purpose was to wow the locals.

👁 MAP P42, B3

📞 220 516 740

www.loreta.cz

Loretánské náměstí 7

adult/child 180/90Kč

🕙 9am-5pm Apr-Oct, 9.30am-4pm Nov-Mar

🚋 22, 23

Santa Casa

The duplicate Santa Casa is in the centre of a courtyard complex, surrounded by cloistered arcades, churches and chapels. The interior is adorned with 17th-century frescoes and reliefs depicting the life of the Virgin Mary, and an ornate silver altar with a wooden effigy of Our Lady of Loreto.

Prague Sun

The eye-popping treasury boasts a star attraction – a dazzling object called the 'Prague Sun'. Studded with 6222 diamonds, it was a gift to the Loreta from Countess Ludmila of Kolowrat. In her will she wrote that the piece must be crafted from her personal collection of diamonds – wedding gifts from her third husband.

Church of the Nativity of Our Lord

Behind the Santa Casa is the Church of the Nativity of Our Lord, built in 1737 to a design by Christoph Dientzenhofer. The claustrophobic interior includes two skeletons of the Spanish saints Felicissima and Marcia, dressed in aristocratic clothing with wax masks concealing their skulls.

The Bearded Lady

At the corner of the courtyard is the unusual Chapel of Our Lady of Sorrows, featuring a crucified bearded lady. She was St Starosta, pious daughter of a Portuguese king who promised her to the king of Sicily against her wishes. After a night of tearful prayers she awoke with a beard, the wedding was called off, and her father had her crucified. She was later made patron saint of the needy and the godforsaken.

★ Top Tips

o The worthwhile audio guide, available in several languages, costs 150Kč.

o Families (two adults and up to five children under 16) can ask for the 370Kč family rate.

o If you'd like to take photos (no flash or tripod allowed), ask for a permit (100Kč).

✖ Take a Break

For a cold beer, head along to **Klášterní Pivovar** (p45), a modern microbrewery that operates on the site of a 17th-century monastic brewery.

Prague Castle & Hradčany Admire the Baroque Beauty of Loreta

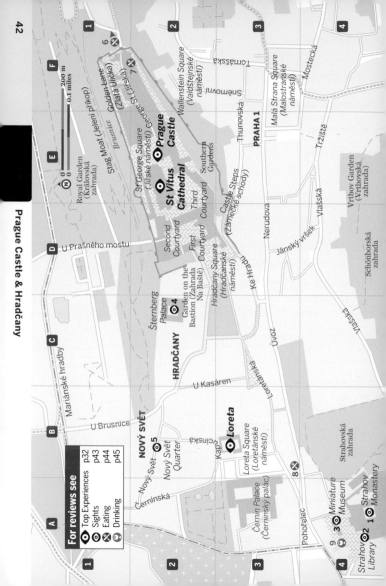

Prague Castle & Hradčany

For reviews see
- ◉ Top Experiences   p32
- ◉ Sights   p43
- ✕ Eating   p44
- 🍷 Drinking   p45

Royal Garden (Královská zahrada)

Stag Moat (Jelení příkop)

Brusnice

Golden Lane (Zlatá ulička)

St George Sq (Jiřská St (Jiřská))

◉ Prague Castle

St George Square (Jiřské náměstí)

◉ St Vitus Cathedral

Southern Gardens

Second Courtyard

Wallenstein Square (Valdštejnské náměstí)

Sněmovní

PRAHA 1

Malá Strana Square (Malostranské náměstí)

Tomášská

Mostecká

First Courtyard

Third Courtyard

Castle Steps (Zámecké schody)

Thunovská

Šternberg Palace

◉4 Garden on the Bastion (Zahrada Na Baště)

Hradčany Square (Hradčanské náměstí)

Ke Hradu

Nerudova

Jánský vršek

Vlašská

Vrtbov Garden (Vrtbovská zahrada)

Schönborská zahrada

Vlašská

Tržiště

Úvoz

U Prašného mostu

Mariánské hradby

HRADČANY

U Kasáren

Loretánská

U Brusnice

NOVÝ SVĚT

Nový Svět Quarter

Kanovnická

◉5

◉ Loreta

Loreta Square (Loretánské náměstí)

Kapucínská

✕8

Černín Palace (Černínský palác)

Černínská

Pohořelec

Strahovská zahrada

Miniature Museum

🍷3

◉ Strahov Monastery

Strahov Library

◉2

◉1

N 0   200 m
0   0.1 miles

Sights

Strahov Monastery
MONASTERY

1 ◉ MAP P42, A4

In 1140 Vladislav II founded Strahov Monastery for the Premonstratensian order. The present monastery buildings, completed in the 17th and 18th centuries, functioned until the communist government closed them down and imprisoned most of the monks; they returned in 1990. The main attraction here is the magnificent Strahov Library (p43).

Inside the main gate is the 1612 **Church of St Roch** (kostel sv Rocha), which is now an art gallery, and the **Church of the Assumption of Our Lady** (kostel Nanebevzetí Panny Marie), built in 1143 and heavily decorated in the 18th century in the baroque style; Mozart is said to have played the organ here. (Strahovský klášter; ☎ 233 107 704; www.strahovskyklaster.cz; Strahovské nádvoří 1; 🚊 22, 23)

Strahov Library
HISTORIC BUILDING

2 ◉ MAP P42, A4

Strahov Library is the largest monastic library in the country, with two magnificent baroque halls dating from the 17th and 18th centuries. You can peek through the doors but, sadly, you can't go into the halls themselves – it was found that fluctuations in humidity caused by visitors' breath were endangering the frescoes. There's also a display of historical curiosities. (Strahovská knihovna; ☎ 233 107 718; www.strahovskyklaster.cz; Strahovské nádvoří 1; adult/child 150/80Kč; ⊙ 9-11.30am & 12.30-5pm; 🚊 22, 23)

Miniature Museum
MUSEUM

3 ◉ MAP P42, A4

Siberian technician Anatoly Konyenko once manufactured tools for microsurgery, but in his spare time he spent 7½ years crafting a pair of golden horseshoes for a flea. See those, as well as the Lord's Prayer inscribed on a single human hair, a grasshoper clutching a violin, and a camel caravan silhouetted in the eye of a needle. Weird but fascinating. (Muzeum Miniatúr; ☎ 233 352 371; www.muzeumminiatur.cz; Strahovské nádvoří II; adult/child 130/70Kč; ⊙9am-5pm; 🚊 22, 23)

Šternberg Palace
GALLERY

4 ◉ MAP P42, C2

The baroque Šternberg Palace is home to the National Gallery's collection of European art from ancient Greece and Rome up to the 18th century, including works by Goya and Rembrandt. Fans of medieval altarpieces will be in heaven, and there are also several Rubens, some Brueghels, and a large collection of Bohemian miniatures.

Pride of the gallery is the glowing *Feast of the Rosary* by Albrecht Dürer, an artist better known for his engravings. Painted in Venice in 1505 as an altarpiece for the church of San Bartolomeo, it was brought to Prague by Rudolf II; in the background, beneath the tree on the right, is the figure of the artist himself. (Šternberský palác; www.ngprague.cz; Hradčanské náměstí 15; incl admission to all National Gallery venues adult/up to 26yr 500Kč/free; 🕙10am-6pm Tue-Sun, to 8pm Wed; 🚋22, 23)

Nový Svět Quarter

AREA

5 🎯 MAP P42, B2

In the 16th century, houses were built for castle staff in an enclave of curving cobblestone streets down the slope north of the Loreta. Today these diminutive cottages have been restored and painted in pastel shades, making the 'New World' quarter a perfect alternative to the castle's crowded Golden Lane. Danish astronomer Tycho Brahe once lived at Nový Svět 1. (🚋22, 23)

Eating

Villa Richter

CZECH €€

6 🍴 MAP P42, F1

Housed in a restored 18th-century villa in the middle of a replanted medieval vineyard, this place is something quite special and not really for the hordes of tourists thronging up and down the Old Castle Steps. The outdoor tables on terraces enjoy one of the finest views in the city, and the restrained menu of classic Czech dishes doesn't disappoint. (📞702 205 108; www.villarichter.cz; Staré zamecké schody 6; mains 345-745Kč; 🕙11am-11pm; Ⓜ️Malostranská)

Lobkowicz Palace Café

CAFE €€

7 🍴 MAP P42, F2

This cafe, housed in the 16th-century Lobkowicz Palace (p36), is the best eatery in the castle complex by an imperial mile. Try to grab one of the tables on the balconies at the back – the view over the city is superb, as are the soups, sandwiches and goulash. The coffee is good too, and service is fast and friendly. (www.lobkowicz.com; Jiřská 3; mains 205-280Kč, 3-course menu 365Kč; 🕙10am-6pm; 📶👶🚋22, 23)

Malý Buddha

ASIAN €

8 🍴 MAP P42, B3

Candlelight, incense and a Buddhist shrine characterise this intimate, rather incongruous Asian tearoom opposite the Swedish embassy. The menu is a blend of Asian influences, with authentic Thai noodles, Chinese rice and Vietnamese soups, many of them vegetarian, and a drinks list that includes ginseng wine, Chinese rose liqueur and all kinds of tea. (📞220 513 894; Úvoz 46; mains 150-300Kč; 🕙noon-10pm Tue-Sun; 🚭; 🚋22, 23)

Getting to Know
Good 'King' Wenceslas

Thanks to British clergyman John Mason Neale, the name 'Wenceslas' is known to English speakers the world over. It was Neale who penned the popular Christmas carol 'Good King Wenceslas' in 1853. Neale was apparently inspired by the tale of a page and his master taking food and firewood to the poor on a freezing day over the Christmas holiday.

However, Neale was either mistaken or consciously exaggerating. Wenceslas ('Václav' in Czech) was never a king, but rather the duke of Bohemia, who from 925 to 929 AD helped bring Christianity to the Czech lands. Now the Czechs' chief patron saint, his image pops up all across town, from St Vitus Cathedral to the Wenceslas Statue on (you guessed it) Wenceslas Square.

Despite his piety, Wenceslas came to an unfortunate end. He was murdered by his brother Boleslav for cosying up to neighbouring Germans.

Drinking

Klášterní Pivovar
Strahov   BREWERY

9 😊 MAP P42, A4

Dominated by two polished copper brewing kettles, this convivial little pub in Strahov Monastery serves up two varieties of its St Norbert beer – *tmavý* (dark), a rich, tarry brew with a creamy head; and *polotmavý* (amber), a full-bodied,

hoppy lager – plus a few seasonal specials. The slightly pricey mains often use the beer as an ingredient.

The modern microbrewery opened in 2000 on the site of a monastic brewery that was in operation from 1628 to 1907. (Strahov Monastery Brewery; 📞233 353 155; www.klasterni-pivovar.cz; Strahovské nádvoří 301; ⏰10am-10pm; 🚋22, 23)

Explore ⊕
Malá Strana & Petřín Hill

Almost too picturesque for its own good, the baroque district of Malá Strana (Little Quarter) tumbles down the hillside between Prague Castle and the river. The focal point here is Malostranské Square, dominated by the green dome of St Nicholas Church. Petřín Hill, topped by a park and faux-but-fun Eiffel Tower, rises south of the square.

The Short List

○ **Petřín Hill (p48)** *Rising opposite the castle, the wooded Petřín has several attractions and is a perfect escape from the tourist crowds.*

○ **Gardens of Malá Strana (p50)** *The secret gardens of this neighbourhood are relaxing oases of green dotted with baroque finery.*

○ **St Nicholas Church (p53)** *One of Europe's finest baroque churches dominates the northern end of Malostranské Square.*

○ **Nerudova (p54)** *Part of the Royal Way, sloping Nerudova street climbs to the castle and is lined with tall baroque townhouses and palaces.*

Getting There & Around

🚋 Take 12, 15, 20, 22 or 23 to Malostranské náměstí, Hellichova or Újezd.

Ⓜ The closest stop is Malostranská on Line A.

Neighbourhood Map on p52

Malá Strana cobblestone street MARCUS LINDSTROM/GETTY IMAGES©

Top Experience
Hike up Petřín Hill

This 318m-high hill is one of Prague's largest green spaces. It's great for quiet, tree-shaded walks and fine views over the 'city of a hundred spires' from the observation deck of a highly convincing Eiffel Tower replica. There were once vineyards here, and a quarry that provided the stone for most of Prague's Romanesque and Gothic buildings. Take the funicular railway up to add a bit of a day-trip feel.

◉ **MAP P52, B3**
🕙 24hr
🚋 Nebozízek, Petřín

Petřín Funicular

First opened in 1891, the **Petřín Funicular Railway** (Lanová draha na Petřín; www.dpp.cz; Újezd; adult/child 32/16Kč; ⊙9am-11.30pm; 🚋9, 12, 15, 20, 22, 23) trundles along 510m of track every 15 minutes from Újezd to the Petřín Lookout Tower, with a stop at Nebozízek.

Petřín Lookout Tower

Some of the best views of Prague – including, on a clear day, the Central Bohemian forests – are from the top of this 62m-tall **tower** (Petřínská rozhledna; 🕿 257 320 112; www.muzeum prahy.cz; Petřínské sady; adult/child 150/80Kč; ⊙10am-10pm Apr-Sep, to 8pm Mar & Oct, to 6pm Nov-Feb; 🚋Petřín), built in 1891 for the Prague Exposition. The Eiffel Tower lookalike has 299 steps (and a lift).

Memorial to the Victims of Communism

The striking **Memorial to the Victims of Communism** (Památník obětem komunismu; cnr Újezd & Vítězná; 🚋9, 12, 15, 20) sculpture shows disintegrating human figures descending a staggered slope. A bronze plaque records the terrible human toll of the communist era: 205,486 arrested, 170,938 driven into exile, 248 executed, 4500 who died in prison, and 327 shot trying to escape.

Mirror Maze

The **Mirror Maze** (Zrcadlové bludiště; www. muzeumprahy.cz; Petřínské sady; adult/child 90/70Kč; ⊙10am-10pm Apr-Sep, to 8pm Mar & Oct, to 6pm Nov-Feb; 🚋Petřín), just below the Lookout Tower, was also built for the 1891 Prague Exposition. The maze of distorting mirrors was based on the Prater in Vienna. There's also, inexplicably, a diorama of the 1648 Battle of Prague.

★ **Top Tips**

o Before heading up the hill, stop at a bakery or supermarket to pick up a picnic. There are lots of benches and places to unfurl a blanket.

o Hiking up Petřín Hill is a pleasant alternative to the funicular and not too strenuous if you follow the winding paths.

o Ride the funicular at night for glittering views of the city.

o Instead of taking the funicular down, consider walking northward through the top of the park towards Strahov Monastery.

✕ **Take a Break**

Restaurant Nebozízek (🕿602 312 739; www.nebozizek. cz; Petřínské sady 411; mains 220-650Kč; ⊙11am-10pm) is located halfway up Petřín Hill's funicular route – it offers wonderful views and is also accessible by foot. **Café Savoy** (p56), not far from the funicular base station, is great for either coffee or lunch.

Walking Tour 🥾

Gardens of Malá Strana

The aristocrats who inhabited Malá Strana in the 17th and 18th centuries sculpted beautiful baroque gardens, many of which are open to the public. From April to October, whenever the sun shines, the neighbourhood's parks and gardens fill with local students toting sketchbooks, young mothers with kids, and business types relaxing on their lunch breaks. Note that from November to March, many of the parks are closed.

Start Gardens Beneath Prague Castle,
Ⓜ Malostranská

End Vrtbov Garden,
Ⓜ Malostranská

Length 2.6km; two hours

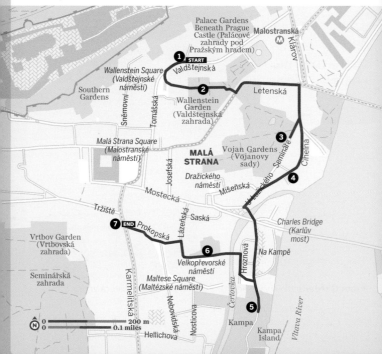

❶ Stroll the Gardens Beneath Prague Castle

The terraced **Gardens Beneath Prague Castle** (Palácové zahrady pod Pražským hradem; www.palacove -zahrady.czadult/child 80/60Kč; ⏱10am-7pm May-Sep, to 6pm Apr & Oct), on the steep southern slopes below the castle, date from the 17th and 18th centuries. Restored in the 1990s, they contain a Renaissance loggia with frescoes of Pompeii and a baroque portal with sundial that cleverly catches the sunlight reflected off a fountain's water.

❷ Admire Wallenstein Garden

Baroque **Wallenstein Garden** (Valdštejnská zahrada; Letenská 10; admission free; ⏱7.30am-6pm Mon-Fri, 10am-6pm Sat & Sun Mar-Oct, to 7pm daily Jun-Sep) is an oasis of peace amid the bustle of Malá Strana. Created for Duke Albrecht of Wallenstein in the 17th century, its finest feature is the huge loggia decorated with scenes from the Trojan Wars, flanked by an enormous fake stalactite grotto dotted with carved grotesque faces.

❸ Hang Out With Locals in Vojan Gardens

While less manicured than most of Malá Strana's parks, **Vojan Gardens** (Vojanovy sady; U Lužického semináře; admission free; ⏱8am-dusk) is a popular spot with locals who like to come here to take a breather with the kids, sit in the sun or even hold summer parties.

❹ Spot an Unusual Fountain

In the open-air plaza in front of the Franz Kafka Museum is the much-photographed David Černý sculpture, **Proudy**. The quirky animatronic sculpture features two men relieving themselves into a puddle shaped like Czechia.

❺ Feel the Breeze at Kampa

Toss a Frisbee, take a load off, or just watch the local hipsters play with their dogs at the leafy riverside park known simply as **Kampa**. It's one of the city's favourite chill-out zones.

❻ Find Inner Peace

The **John Lennon Wall** (Velkopřevorské náměstí) is a memorial graffiti wall to the former Beatle who became a pacifist hero for young Czechs; his image was painted on this wall opposite the French Embassy, along with political graffiti.

❼ Discover a Secret Garden

The 'secret' **Vrtbov Garden** (Vrtbovská zahrada; www.vrtbovska. cz; Karmelitská 25; adult/concession 80/60Kč; ⏱10am-6pm Apr-Oct), hidden along an alley at the corner of Tržiště and Karmelitská, was built in 1720 for the Earl of Vrtba, the senior chancellor of Prague Castle. It's a formal baroque garden with baroque statues of Roman mythological figures by Matthias Braun.

Malá Strana & Petřín Hill

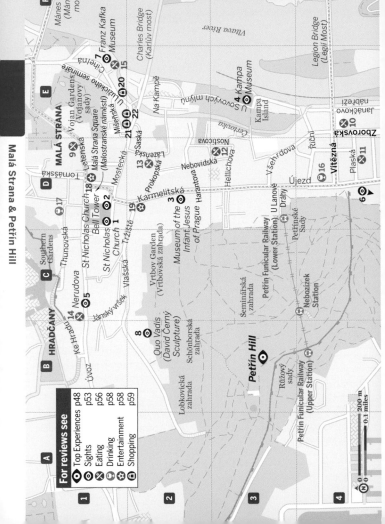

For reviews see

◉ Top Experiences	p48
◉ Sights	p53
✕ Eating	p56
✕ Drinking	p58
✿ Entertainment	p58
⊡ Shopping	p59

HRADČANY

MALÁ STRANA

Franz Kafka Museum

Vltava River

Charles Bridge (Karlův most)

Mánes Bridge (Mánesův most)

Legion Bridge (Legií Most)

Kampa Museum

Kampa Island

Vojan Gardens (Vojanovy sady)

Cihelná

U Sovových mlýnů

Certovka

Na Kampě

Janáčkovo nábřeží

Zborovská

Říční

Vítězná

Plaská

Újezd

Všehrdova

Hellichova

Harantova

Nebovidská

Nosticova

Lazeňská

Prokopská

Saská

Pštrossova

Mostecká

Míšeňská

Malá Strana Square (Malostranské náměstí)

Letenská

Tomášská

St Nicholas Church Bell Tower

St Nicholas Church

Zámecké schody

Vrtbov Garden (Vrtbovská zahrada)

Museum of the Infant Jesus of Prague

Karmelitská

Tržiště

Vlašská

Jánský vršek

Ke Hradu

Úvoz

Nerudova

Thunovská

Southern Gardens

Petřín Funicular Railway (Lower Station)

U Lanové Dráhy

Petřínské Sady

Nebozízek Station

Seminářská zahrada

Petřín Hill

Růžový sady

Petřín Funicular Railway (Upper Station)

Lobkovická zahrada

Schönborská zahrada

Quo Vadis (David Černý Sculpture)

200 m
0.1 miles

Sights

St Nicholas Church
CHURCH

1 MAP P52, D1

Malá Strana is dominated by the huge green cupola of St Nicholas Church, one of Central Europe's finest baroque buildings. (Don't confuse it with the other Church of St Nicholas on Old Town Square.) On the ceiling, Johann Kracker's 1770 *Apotheosis of St Nicholas* is Europe's largest fresco (clever trompe l'oeil techniques have made the painting merge almost seamlessly with the architecture). (Kostel sv Mikuláše; www.stnicholas.cz; Malostranské náměstí 38; adult/child 100/40Kč; ⏰9am-5pm Feb-Oct, to 4pm Nov-Jan; 🚋12, 15, 20, 22, 23)

St Nicholas Church Bell Tower
TOWER

2 MAP P52, D1

During the communist era, the bell tower of St Nicholas Church was used to spy on the nearby American embassy – on the way up you can still see a small, white cast-iron urinal that was installed for the use of the watchers. Today it provides visitors with a grand view over Malá Strana and Charles Bridge. (📞725 847 927; http://en.muzeumprahy.cz/prague-towers; Malostranské náměstí 29; adult/child 100/70Kč; ⏰10am-10pm Apr-Sep, to 8pm Mar & Oct, to 6pm Nov-Feb; 🚋12, 15, 20, 22, 23)

Museum of the Infant Jesus of Prague
CHURCH

3 MAP P52, D2

The rather plain-looking Church of Our Lady Victorious (kostel Panny Marie Vítězné), built in 1613, has on its central altar a 47cm-tall waxwork figure of the baby Jesus, brought from Spain in 1628 and known as the Infant Jesus of Prague (Pražské Jezulátko, or sometimes known by its Italian name, Babino di Praga). At the back of the church is a tiny museum displaying a selection of the frocks used to dress the Infant. (Muzeum Pražského Jezulátka; 📞257 533 646; www.pragjesu.cz; Karmelitská 9; admission free; ⏰8.30am-7pm Mon-Sat, to 8pm Sun; 🚋12, 15, 20, 22, 23)

Kampa Museum
GALLERY

4 MAP P52, E3

Established by art collectors Meda and Jan Mládek and housed in a renovated mill building, this excellent gallery is devoted to 20th-century and contemporary art from Central Europe. The highlights of the permanent exhibition are extensive collections of bronzes by cubist sculptor Otto Gutfreund and paintings by František Kupka – the most impressive canvas is Kupka's *Cathedral,* a pleated mass of blue and red diagonals. The museum also hosts temporary exhibitions of the highest quality. (Muzeum Kampa; 📞257 286 147; www.museumkampa.

cz; U Sovových mlýnů 2; adult/concession 320/160Kč; ⏰10am-6pm; 🚊12, 15, 20, 22, 23)

Nerudova   STREET

5 ◎ MAP P52, C1

Following the tourist crowds downhill from the castle via Ke Hradu, you will arrive at Nerudova, architecturally the most important street in Malá Strana – most of its old Renaissance facades were 'baroquefied' in the 18th century. It's named after the Czech poet Jan Neruda (famous for his short stories, *Tales of Malá Strana)*, who lived at the **House of the Two Suns** (dům U dvou sluncú; Nerudova 47) from 1845 to 1857.

The **House of the Golden Horseshoe** (dům U zlaté podkovy; Nerudova 34) is named after the relief of St Wenceslas above the doorway – his horse was said to be shod with gold. From 1765 Josef of Bretfeld made his **Bretfeld Palace** (Nerudova 33) a social hotspot, entertaining the likes of Mozart and Casanova. The baroque **Church of Our Lady of Unceasing Succour** (kostel Panny Marie ustavičné pomoci; Nerudova 24) was a theatre from 1834 to 1837, and staged Czech plays during the Czech National Revival.Built in 1566, **St John of Nepomuk House** (Nerudova 18) is adorned with the image of one of Bohemia's patron saints, while the **House at the Three Fiddles** (dům U tří houslíček; Nerudova 12), a Gothic building reconstructed in Renaissance style during the 17th century, once belonged to a family of violin makers. Most of the buildings bear typical Prague house signs. (🚊12, 15, 20, 22, 23)

Národopisné muzeum   MUSEUM

6 ◎ MAP P52, D4

One of Prague's least visited museums is a joy for those into a bit of Slavic colour. Housed in a renovated summer palace, the National Museum's ethnographic collection does a good

---

Give Me a Sign

Until numbering was introduced in the 18th century, exotic house names and signs were the only way of identifying individual Prague buildings. This practice came to a halt in 1770, when it was banned by the city councillors.

More such-named houses and signs survive on **Nerudova** than along any other Prague street. As you head downhill look out for At the Two Suns (No 47), the Golden Horseshoe (No 34), the Three Fiddles (No 12), the Red Eagle (No 6) and the Devil (No 4). Other signs include St Wenceslas on horseback (No 34), a golden key (No 27) and a golden goblet (No 16).

MONIKAM.1/SHUTTERSTOCK ©

Interior dome of St Nicholas Church (p53)

job of providing an overview of traditional Czech folk culture and art, including music, costume, farming methods and handicrafts. It's also a venue for folk concerts and workshops demonstrating traditional crafts. The garden cafe is an oasis of peace in summer. (Ethnographical Museum; ☎257 214 806; www.nm.cz; Kinského zahrada 98; adult/child 70/40Kč; ⏰10am-6pm Tue-Sun; 🚋9, 12, 15, 20)

Franz Kafka Museum   MUSEUM

7 ◎ MAP P52, E1

This much-hyped and slightly overpriced exhibition on the life and work of Prague's most famous literary son, entitled 'City of K', explores the intimate relationship between the writer and the city

that shaped him, through the use of original letters, photographs, quotations, period newspapers and publications, and video and sound installations. (Muzeum Franzy Kafky; ☎257 535 373; www.kafkamuseum.cz; Cihelná 2b; adult/child 260/180Kč; ⏰10am-6pm; Ⓜ Malostranská)

Quo Vadis (David Černý Sculpture)   MONUMENT

8 ◎ MAP P52, B2

This bronze Trabant (an East German car) on four human legs is a David Černý tribute to the 4000 East Germans who occupied the garden of the then West German embassy in 1989, before being granted political asylum and leaving their Trabants behind. You

Kafka's Neighbourhood

'Someone must have been telling lies about Josef K, for without having done anything wrong, he was arrested one fine morning' – that opening line in Franz Kafka's *The Trial* (1925) is widely considered to be among the greatest in world literature. The words are also a testament to Prague's disorientating nature, and in the writer's home city it's hard not to be moved by his genius. Of course, it's simple to pay tribute to Kafka by visiting his birthplace or grave, but true fans will want to use the opportunity to delve more into the novelist's complex relationship with Prague, which he complained was small and claustrophobic but got under your skin. The **Franz Kafka Museum** (p55) is just the place.

can see the sculpture through the fence behind the German embassy. To find it, head uphill along Vlašská, turn left into a children's park, and left again. (www.davidcerny.cz; Vlašská 19; 🚊12, 15, 20, 22, 23)

Eating

Augustine CZECH €€€

9 🍴 MAP P52, D1

Hidden away in the historic Augustine Hotel (check out the ceiling fresco in the bar), this sophisticated yet relaxed restaurant is well worth seeking out. The menu ranges from down-to-earth but delicious dishes such as pork cheeks braised in the hotel's own St Thomas beer, to inventive dishes built around fresh Czech produce. The two-course business lunch costs 380Kč. (📞266 112 280; www.augustine-restaurant.cz; Letenská 12; mains 350-590Kč, 4-course tasting menu 1350Kč; ⏰7am-11pm; 🛜; 🚊12, 15, 20, 22)

Café Savoy EUROPEAN €€

10 🍴 MAP P52, E4

The Savoy is a beautifully restored Austrian-era cafe, with smart, suited waitstaff and a Viennese-style menu of hearty soups, salads, roast meats and schnitzels. It's also just a characterful place for coffee and cake and there's a superb wine list (ask the staff for recommendations). (📞731 136 144; http://cafesavoy.ambi.cz; Vítězná 5; mains 258-785Kč; ⏰8am-10.30pm Mon-Fri, 9am-10.30pm Sat & Sun; 🛜; 🚊9, 22, 23)

Ichnusa Botega Bistro ITALIAN €€

11 🍴 MAP P52, D4

'Ichnusa' is the ancient name for Sardinia, which is where owner Antonella Pranteddu sources all of the meats, cheeses and wines he serves in this inviting, family-run affair, Eastern Europe's only Sardi resto. Exotic dishes such as *malloreddus* (a type of gnocchi), spaghetti *alla bottarga* (dried roe spaghetti) and grilled swordfish populate the menu, though (mercifully) Sardinia's donkey specialities don't feature. (☎605 375 012; Plaská 5; mains 265-550Kč; ⊙11am-10pm Mon-Fri, from 4pm Sat; ☎; 🚊12, 15, 20, 22, 23)

U Modré Kachničky   CZECH €€€

13 ✖ MAP P52, D3

A plush 1930s-style hunting lodge hidden away on a quiet side street, 'At the Blue Duckling' is a pleasantly old-fashioned place with quiet, candlelit nooks perfect for a romantic dinner. Traditional Bohemian duck dishes such as roast duck with nut stuffing and potato pancakes are the speciality. The venison also comes highly recom-

mended, and there are a couple of vegetarian options. (☎257 320 308; www.umodrekachnicky.cz; Nebovidská 6; mains 500-640Kč; ⊙noon-4pm & 6.30-11.30pm; ☎; 🚊12, 15, 20, 22, 23)

Cukrkávalimonáda   EUROPEAN €

13 ✖ MAP P52, D2

A cute little cafe-cum-bistro that combines minimalist 21st-century styling with impressive Renaissance-era painted timber roof beams, CKL offers fresh, homemade pastas, frittatas, ciabattas, salads and pancakes (sweet and savoury) by day and a slightly more sophisticated menu in the early evening. There's also a good choice of breakfasts: ham and eggs, croissants and yoghurt. The hot chocolate is a real treat. (☎257 225 396; www.

U Malého Glena (p59)

cukrkavalimonada.com; Lázeňská 7; mains 150-250Kč; ◎9am-7pm; 🚊12, 15, 20, 22, 23)

Vegan's Prague

VEGAN €€

14 ✕ MAP P52, C1

For vegans visiting the castle or Malá Strana, this clean-cut, 1st-floor restaurant is a godsend. Under heavy Renaissance beams, enjoy curries, veggie burgers, fruit dumplings and meat-and-dairy-free versions of Czech favourites, plus lots of teas, juices and organic coffees. The tiny, one-table terrace has spellbinding views of the castle, but you can bet someone got there before you. (📞735 171 313; www.vegansprague.cz; Nerudova 36; mains 239-279Kč; ◎11.30am-9.30pm; 🛜✎; 🚊12, 15, 20, 22, 23)

Hergetova Cihelna

INTERNATIONAL €€

15 ✕ MAP P52, E1

Housed in a converted 18th-century *cihelna* (brickworks), this long-established restaurant enjoys one of Prague's hottest locations, with a riverside terrace offering sweeping views of Charles Bridge (great in warm weather). The menu is as sweeping as the view, ranging from fish and chips to Czech game dishes, spelt risotto and veal schnitzel. It also serves some better-than-most desserts. (📞296 826 103; www.kampagroup.com; Cihelná 2b; mains 365-595Kč; lunch menu 185-285Kč; ◎11.30am-4pm & 6pm-midnight; 🛜🚼; Ⓜ Malostranská)

Drinking

Klub Újezd

BAR

16 🚇 MAP P52, D4

Klub Újezd is one of Prague's many 'alternative' bars, spread over three floors (DJs in the cellar, and a cafe upstairs) and filled with a fascinating collection of original art and weird wrought-iron sculptures. Clamber onto a two-tonne bar stool in the grungy street-level bar, and sip on a beer beneath a scaly, fire-breathing sea monster. (📞251 510 873; www.klubujezd.cz; Újezd 18; ◎2pm-4am; 🚊9, 12, 15, 20, 22, 23)

U Hrocha

BEER HALL

17 🚇 MAP P52, D1

Just around the corner from the British Embassy, this old Malá Strana boozer hasn't changed much since the grotty days of the worker's republic, and is still serving its Urquell and basic soak-up food at simple wooden benches. It's normally inhabited by locals, so who knows, you might even meet the British ambassador here chatting about Brexit. (📞257 533 389; Thunovská 2; ◎noon-11pm; 🚊12, 15, 20, 22, 23)

Entertainment

Malostranská Beseda

LIVE MUSIC

18 ✪ MAP P52, D1

A legendary Prague venue, Malá Strana's four-storey entertainment palace boasts a fabled music club on the 2nd floor, with a lively roster of Czech acts old and new, famous and 'keep-the-day-job'. There's also a low-key art gallery on the top floor, a bar and restaurant on the ground floor, and a big beer hall in the basement serving Urquell beer and snacks. (📞257 409 104; www.malostranska-beseda.cz; Malostranské náměstí 21; ⊙bar 4pm-1am, box office 5-9pm Mon-Sat, to 8pm Sun; 🚊12, 15, 20, 22, 23)

U Malého Glena
LIVE MUSIC

19 🌟 MAP P52, D2

American-owned 'Little Glen's' has been around since 1995 and is *the* venue for hard-swinging local jazz or blues bands who play every night in the cramped and steamy stone-vaulted cellar. There are Sunday-night jam sessions where amateurs are welcome (as long as you're good!) – it's a small venue, so get here early if you want to see as well as hear the band. (📞257 531 717; www.malyglen.cz; Karmelitská 23; ⊙10am-2am Sun-Thu, to 3am Fri & Sat, music from 8.30pm; 📶; 🚊12, 15, 20, 22, 23)

Shopping

Shakespeare & Sons
BOOKS

20 🔒 MAP P52, E1

Though its shelves groan with a formidable range of literature in English, French and German, this is more than just a bookshop (with Prague's best range of titles on Eastern European history) – it's a congenial literary hang-out with knowledgeable staff, occasional author events and a cool downstairs space for sitting and reading. (📞257 531 894; www.shakes.cz; U Lužického semináře 10; ⊙11am-8pm; 🚊12, 15, 20, 22, 23)

Marionety Truhlář
ARTS & CRAFTS

21 🔒 MAP P52, E2

This palace of puppetry stocks traditional marionettes from more than 40 workshops around Czechia, as well as offering DIY puppet kits, courses on puppet-making, and the chance to order a custom-made marionette in your own (or anyone else's) likeness. (📞602 689 918; www.marionety.com; U Lužického semináře 5; ⊙10am-7pm; 🚊12, 15, 20, 22, 23)

Artěl
DESIGN

22 🔒 MAP P52, E2

Traditional Bohemian glass-making meets modern design in this stylish shop founded by US designer Karen Feldman. In addition to hand-blown designer crystal, you can find a range of vintage and modern items of Czech design, from jewellery and ceramics to toys and stationery. (📞251 554 008; www.artelglass.com; U Lužickeho semináře 7; ⊙10am-8pm; 🚊12, 15, 20, 22, 23)

Walking Tour 🥾

Beer & Culture in Smíchov

Standing in contrast to the fairy-tale historic sphere of castles and royal gardens, working-class Smíchov is a mainly industrial district on the Vltava's western bank. With its vibrant contemporary-art scene and unpretentious bars, the slightly gritty neighbourhood offers an authentic taste of Czech life, though its character is slowly changing with the construction of modern office complexes and an influx of new businesses.

Start Jazz Dock;
🚋 Arbesovo náměstí

End MeetFactory;
🚋 Lihovar

Length 6.3km; two hours

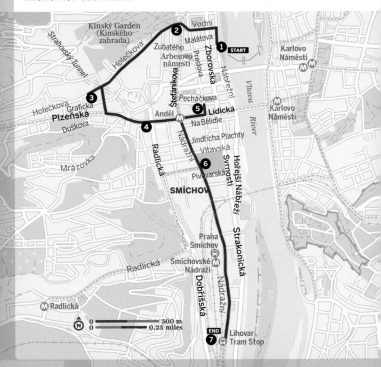

❶ Jazz on the River

Jazz Dock (www.jazzdock.cz; Janáčkovo nábřeží 2; tickets 200-400Kč; ☺3pm-4am Mon-Thu, from 1pm Fri-Sun Apr-Sep, 5pm-4am Mon-Thu, from 3pm Fri-Sun Oct-Mar), Smíchov's riverside jazz venue, is a step up from the typical Prague club, with clean, modern decor and a romantic view over the Vltava. It draws some of the best international acts.

❷ Avant-Garde Theatre at Švandovo Divadlo

The funky **Švandovo Divadlo** (Švandovo Theatre in Smíchov; www.svandovodivadlo.cz; Štefánikova 57; tickets 250-400Kč; ☺box office 2-8pm Mon-Fri, plus 2hr before performances Sat & Sun) stages avant-garde dramatic pieces, many with English subtitles, and acoustic music performances. It also hosts art exhibits and events.

❸ Modern Art at Futura

The **Futura Gallery** (Centre for Contemporary Art Futura; www.futuraproject.cz; Holečkova 49; admission by donation; ☺11am-6pm Wed-Sun) is home to *Brown-nosers* (2003) by David Černý: stick your head inside the statue's backside to see a video of former Czech president Václav Klaus and the National Gallery's director feeding each other baby food.

❹ Czech Food at Zlatý Klas

Cosy Pilsner Urquell restaurant **Zlatý Klas** (www.zlatyklas.cz; Plzeňská 9; mains 195-300Kč; ☺11am-11pm Sun-Thu, 11.30am-1am Fri & Sat) is beloved for its hearty, well-prepared Czech cuisine and tank beer.

❺ Dancing at the 'Bulldog'

A beer-fuelled, dance-till-you-drop joint, **Hospoda U Buldoka** (www.ubuldoka.cz; Preslova 1; ☺11am-midnight Mon-Thu, to 1am Fri, 3pm-midnight Sat, 3pm-10pm Sun) is a great place to drink, and to let your hair down.

❻ Beer at Staropramen the Brewery

To soak up some of Smíchov's down-to-earth charm pull up a barstool at **Na Verandách** (www.phnaverandach.cz; Nádražní 84; mains 160-300Kč; ☺11am-midnight Mon-Sat, to 11pm Sun), housed in the Staropramen Brewery.

❼ 'MeetFactory' Events

For cutting-edge film screenings, concerts, theatrical performances and art installations, check out David Černý's **MeetFactory** (www.meetfactory.cz; Ke Sklárně 15; admission free; ☺1-8pm, varies according to event).

Explore 🧭
Jewish Museum & Josefov

Peaceful Josefov is the site of the former Jewish ghetto – the physical, cultural and spiritual home to the city's Jewish population for nearly 800 years. While many Jews left the quarter when it was renovated in the early 20th century (and tens of thousands were killed in the Holocaust), the surviving synagogues and cemetery make up the popular Jewish Museum.

The Short List

○ *Old Jewish Cemetery (p66)* One of the most atmospheric spots in all Prague with its crooked gravestones and Hebrew-inscribed tombs.

○ *Old-New Synagogue (p69)* The oldest working synagogue on the Continent is wreathed in myths and legends.

○ *Spanish Synagogue (p65)* The most beautiful of the Josefov synagogues now houses a museum.

○ *Gurmet Pasáž Dlouhá (p75)* There's artisan fare galore at this food court in an old art-deco arcade.

○ *Museum of Decorative Arts (p69)* Newly renovated, one of Prague's best museums focuses on Czech design.

Getting There & Around

🚋 Lines 2, 17, 18 to Staroměstská; lines 6, 8, 15, 26 to Dlouhá třída.

Ⓜ Line A to Staroměstská.

Neighbourhood Map on p68

Maisel Synagogue (p65) CHRISDORNEY/SHUTTERSTOCK ©

Top Experience 📷
Gain Insight at the Jewish Museum

Prague's Jewish Museum is among the city's most visited sights. It was established in 1906 to preserve artefacts from the quarter after it was razed and renovated in the late-19th and early-20th centuries. Exhibits are scattered among a handful of synagogues, and focus on Jewish life and traditions. Highlights include the Pinkas Synagogue and its memorial to Czech and Moravian Jews killed in the Holocaust.

◉ MAP P68, B3

www.jewishmuseum.cz

Maiselova 15

adult/child 350/250Kč, incl Old-New Synagogue 500/350Kč

🕑 9am-6pm Sun-Fri Apr-Oct, to 4.30pm Nov-Mar

Ⓜ Staroměstská

Klaus Synagogue & Ceremonial Hall

Both the baroque **Klaus Synagogue** and the nearby **Ceremonial Hall** contain exhibits on Jewish health and burial traditions and will be of most interest to historians or devout visitors.

Maisel Synagogue

Mordechai Maisel was mayor of the Jewish quarter under the liberal rule of Emperor Rudolf II during the 16th century. He was also the richest man in the city of Prague, and in addition to various public works, he paid for this **synagogue** to be built for his private use. Today it houses rotating exhibitions.

Pinkas Synagogue

Built in 1535, this **synagogue** was used for worship until 1941. It's now a moving Holocaust memorial, its walls inscribed with the names, birthdates and dates of disappearance of 77,297 Czech Jews. Also here is a poignant exhibition of drawings made by children held at the Terezín concentration camp (north of Prague) during WWII.

Spanish Synagogue

Considered the most beautiful of the museum's synagogues, this 19th-century Moorish-style **building** (pictured left) boasts an ornate interior, an exhibition on recent Jewish history and a handy bookshop.

★ **Top Tips**

○ Queues for tickets are generally shortest at the Spanish Synagogue.

○ Visit the Old Jewish Cemetery early or late in order to find it at its most peaceful.

○ Men must cover their heads before entering the Old-New Synagogue. Bring a hat or buy a paper yarmulke at the entrance.

✗ **Take a Break**

For a good pint of beer in the vicinity of the Spanish Synagogue, head to corner pub **V Kolkovně** (p72).

Jewish Museum & Josefov Gain Insight at the Jewish Museum

Top Experience 📷
Wander the Old Jewish Cemetery

City authorities once insisted that deceased Jews be interred only here – nowhere else – so by the time this cemetery stopped taking new burials in 1787 it was full to bursting. Today it holds more than 12,000 tombstones, though as the Jewish Museum points out, many more than that are buried here. Be aware that conditions at this popular attraction sometimes feel almost as crowded for the living as for the dead.

 MAP P68, B3

www.jewishmuseum.cz

Pinkas Synagogue, Široká 3

included in admission to Prague Jewish Museum

🕙9am-6pm Apr-Oct, to 4.30pm Nov-Mar

Ⓜ️Staroměstská

Rabbi Loew's Tomb

Sometimes called 'the Jewish hero of the Czechs', Rabbi Judah Loew ben Bezalel (1525–1609) was a respected scholar and the chief rabbi of Bohemia in the 16th century. Perhaps more importantly to Czech people, he's part of a legend surrounding the creation of the Golem, a creature he supposedly built from clay to protect the Jewish people living in Prague's ghetto.

Mordechai Maisel's Tomb

This tomb honours a philanthropist with some incredibly deep pockets. In addition to serving as a Jewish leader in the 16th century, Maisel was the city's wealthiest citizen. He paid for the construction of new buildings in the ghetto, had the roads paved, commissioned the Maisel Synagogue (p65) for his own private use and even lent money to Emperor Rudolf II.

David Gans' Tomb

A noted German historian and astronomer, Gans came to Prague in part to hear the lectures of Rabbi Loew. He's perhaps most famous for his association with Tycho Brahe, who asked Gans to translate the Alphonsine Tables from Hebrew to German.

Joseph Solomon Delmedigo's Tomb

Another impressive Jewish intellectual represented in the cemetery is Joseph Solomon Delmedigo, who was both a physician and a philosopher. He studied and worked all over Europe before finally settling in Prague in 1648 to write various scientific texts.

★ Top Tips

o Entry to the cemetery is included in the general Jewish Museum admission ticket.

o Arrive early as the cemetery gets increasingly busy as the day goes on.

o Remember that you're in a cemetery – always be careful where you step.

✕ Take a Break

Stylish **Mistral Café** (p72) is a short walk from the cemetery and is great for coffee or food.

Also nearby is **U Rudolfina** (☎222 328 758; Křižovnická 10; ⊙11am-10pm; Ⓜ Staroměstská), a down-to-earth local pub with some of the city's best Pilsner Urquell.

Jewish Museum & Josefov

For reviews see
- Top Experiences p64
- Sights p69
- Eating p72
- Drinking p74
- Entertainment p75
- Shopping p75

Čech Bridge (Čechův most)

Vltava River

200 m
0.1 miles

Intercontinental Hotel

Dvořákovo nábřeží

Dušní

U Milosrdných

JOSEFOV

Pařížská

17.listopadu

Rudolfinum

Dvořákovo nábřeží

Bílkova

Kozí

Kozí

Elišky Krásnohorské

Eliščiny

Convent of St Agnes 3

Haštalské náměstí

Rámová

U Obecního dvora

Haštalská

Rybná

Rybná

Benediktská

Masná

Masná

Masná

Dlouhá

Kotva

Prague Wheelchair Users Organisation

Rybná

Jakubská

Malá Štupartská

Týn Courtyard (Týnský dvůr)

Týnská

Týnská ulička

Dlouhá

Old Town Square (Staroměstské náměstí)

Dušní

Salvátorská

Pařížská

Jáchymova

Žatecká

Kaprova

Maiselova

Široká

Valentinská

Staroměstská

Křižovnická

Jan Palach Square (náměstí Jana Palacha)

PRAHA 1

Franz Kafka Monument 5

Old-New Synagogue 1

Museum of Decorative Arts

Červená

Jewish Museum

Old Jewish Cemetery

Veleslavínova

V Kolkovně

7

8

12

11 16

10 15

14

6

9

2

4

13

Sights

Old-New Synagogue

SYNAGOGUE

1 MAP P68, B3

Completed around 1270, this is Europe's oldest working synagogue and one of Prague's earliest Gothic buildings. You step down into it because it pre-dates the raising of Staré Město's street level in medieval times to guard against floods. Men must cover their heads (bring a hat or take one of the paper yarmulkes handed out at the entrance). Although it's one of the seven Jewish monuments that make up the Prague Jewish Museum, entry isn't included in the museum's general admission ticket.

Around the central chamber are an entry hall, a winter prayer hall and the room from which women watch the men-only services. The interior, with a pulpit surrounded by a 15th-century wrought-iron grill, looks much as it would have 500 years ago. The 17th-century scriptures on the walls were recovered from beneath a later 'restoration'. On the eastern wall is the Holy Ark that holds the Torah scrolls. In a glass case at the rear, little light bulbs beside the names of the prominent deceased are lit on their death days. (Staronová synagóga; ☏222 749 211; www.jewishmuseum. cz; Červená 2; adult/child 200/140Kč; ☉9am-6pm Sun-Fri Apr-Oct, to 4.30pm Nov-Mar; 🚊17)

Museum of Decorative Arts

MUSEUM

2 MAP P68, A3

This museum opened in 1900 as part of a European movement to encourage a return to the aesthetic values sacrificed to the Industrial Revolution. Once a graceful old museum packed with Czech glass, furniture, tapestries and period clothing, the whole thing was completely renovated and

Golem City

Tales of golems, or servants created from clay, date back to early Judaism. However, the most famous such mythical creature belonged to 16th-century Prague's Rabbi Loew, of the Old-New Synagogue. Loew is said to have used mud from the Vltava's banks to create a golem to protect the Prague ghetto. However, left alone one Sabbath, the creature ran amok and Rabbi Loew was forced to rush out of a service and remove the magic talisman that kept it moving. He then carried the lifeless body into the synagogue's attic, where some insist it remains. In 1915 Gustav Meyrink's novel *Der Golem* reprised the story and brought it into the European mainstream.

Jewish-Themed Tours

The experts on Jewish Prague, **Wittmann Tours** (☏222 252 472; www.wittmann-tours. com; Novotného lávka 5; tour per person 1100Kč; ☉Josefov tours 9.30am & 2pm Sun-Fri mid-Mar–Dec; ☒2, 17, 18) offer a high-quality three-hour walking tour of Josefov and seven-hour day trips to Terezín (1700Kč per person), daily May to October, four times a week April, November and December. Private tours are also available.

brought firmly into the 21st century (a shame, some say) at the end of the last decade. At the time of writing the building was still only home to temporary shows, with the permanent exhibition yet to be reinstalled. (Umělecko-průmyslové muzeum; ☏251 093 111; www.upm.cz; 17 listopadu 2; adult/child 300/150Kč; ☉10am-8pm Tue, to 6pm Wed-Sun; ☒1, 2, 17, 18)

Convent of St Agnes   GALLERY

 3 ◉ MAP P68, E1

In the northeastern corner of Staré Město is the former Convent of St Agnes, Prague's oldest surviving Gothic building. The 1st-floor rooms hold the National Gallery's permanent collection of medieval and early Renaissance art (1200–1550) from Bohemia and Central Europe, a treasure house

of glowing Gothic altar paintings and polychrome religious sculptures.

In 1234 the Franciscan Order of the Poor Clares was founded by Přemysl king Wenceslas I, who made his sister Anežka (Agnes) the first abbess of the convent. Agnes was beatified in the 19th century and, with hardly accidental timing, Pope John Paul II canonised her as St Agnes of Bohemia just weeks before the revolutionary events of November 1989. In the 16th century the convent was handed over to the Dominicans, and after Joseph II dissolved the monasteries it became a squatters' paradise. It is only since the 1980s that the complex has been restored and renovated. In addition to the art gallery and the 13th-century cloister, you can visit the French Gothic **Church of the Holy Saviour**, which contains the tombs of St Agnes and Wenceslas I's Queen Cunegund. Alongside this is the smaller **Church of St Francis**, where Wenceslas I is buried; part of its ruined nave now serves as a chilly concert hall. The gallery is fully wheelchair-accessible, and the ground-floor cloister has a tactile presentation of 12 casts of medieval sculptures with explanatory text in Braille. Tickets are valid for 10 days. (Klášter sv Anežky; ☏224 810 628; www.ngprague.cz; U Milosrdných 17; admission to all National Gallery venues adult/up to 26yr 500Kč/free; ☉10am-6pm Tue-Sun; ☒6, 8, 15, 26)

Rudolfinum
HISTORIC BUILDING

4 MAP P68, A3

Presiding over **Jan Palach Square** (náměstí Jana Palacha; 🚋17, 18) is the Rudolfinum, home to the Czech Philharmonic Orchestra. This and the National Theatre, both designed by architects Josef Schulz and Josef Zítek, are considered Prague's finest neo-Renaissance buildings. Completed in 1884, the Rudolfinum served as the seat of the Czechoslovak Parliament between the wars, and as the administrative offices of the occupying Nazis during WWII.

The impressive Dvořák Hall (p75), its stage dominated by a vast organ, is one of the main concert venues for the **Prague Spring festival** (Pražské jaro; ☎box office 277 012 677, programme 257 310 414; www.festival.cz; ⏰May). The northern part of the complex houses the **Galerie Rudolfinum** (☎770 100 767; www.galerierudolfinum.cz; Alšovo nábřeží 12; admission free; ⏰10am-6pm Tue-Sun; Ⓜ Staroměstská). There's also a cafe with tables ranged among the Corinthian pillars of the Column Hall. (☎227 059 227; www.rudolfinum.cz; Alšovo nábřeží 12; Ⓜ Staroměstská)

Franz Kafka Monument
MONUMENT

5 MAP P68, C3

Commissioned by Prague's Franz Kafka Society in 2003, Jaroslav Róna's unusual sculpture of a mini-Kafka riding on the shoulders of a giant empty suit was based

Old-New Synagogue (p69)

RUSLAN KALNITSKY/GETTY IMAGES ©

on the writer's story *Description of a Struggle,* in which the author explores a fantasy landscape from the shoulders of 'an acquaintance' (who may be another aspect of the author's personality). Touch Kafka's well-polished feet for luck. (cnr Vězeňská & Dušní; M Staroměstská)

Eating

Lokál
CZECH €

6 🍴 MAP P68, F2

Take a classic Czech beer hall (albeit with cool retro-modern styling), excellent *tankové pivo* (tanked Pilsner Urquell), a daily-changing menu of traditional Bohemian dishes and throw in some unusually smiling, efficient, friendly service and you have Lokál. The combination has been so successful that the place is always busy and the concept has been copied across Prague in recent years. (☑ 734 283 874; www.lokal-dlouha.ambi.cz; Dlouhá 33; mains 129-225Kč; ⏰ 11am-1am Mon-Sat, to midnight Sun; 🛜; 🚊 6, 8, 15, 26)

Field
CZECH €€€

7 🍴 MAP P68, D1

This Michelin-starred restaurant is unfussy and fun. The decor is an amusing art-meets-agriculture blend of never-used farmyard implements and minimalist chic, while the chef creates painterly presentations from the finest of local produce along with freshly foraged herbs and edible flowers. You'll have to book at least a couple of weeks in advance to have a chance of a table. (☑ 222 316 999; www.fieldrestaurant.cz; U Milosrdných 12; mains 640-690Kč, 10-course tasting menu 3600Kč; ⏰ 10am-2.30pm & 6-10.30pm Mon-Fri, noon-3pm & 6-10.30pm Sat & Sun; 🛜; 🚊 17)

V Kolkovně
CZECH €€

8 🍴 MAP P68, D3

Operated by the Pilsner Urquell Brewery, V Kolkovně is a stylish, modern take on the traditional Prague pub, with decor by Czech designers, and fancier versions of classic Czech dishes such as goulash, roast duck and beef sirloin, as well as the odd intruder such as salmon and lamb chops. All washed down with an unsurpassed Urquell beer, of course. (☑ 224 819 701; www.vkolkovne.cz; V Kolkovně 8; mains 295-695Kč; ⏰ 11am-midnight; 🛜; M Staroměstská)

Mistral Café
BISTRO €

9 🍴 MAP P68, A4

Arguably the coolest bistro in the Old Town is frequented by local office workers and the odd student who all come to enjoy well-prepared food in a pleasant dining space. The menu runs all the way from kick-starting breakfasts to full-blown dinners. Unusual dishes such as fish and chips, linguine with goats cheese, and tofu make this a place worth seeking out. Best at breakfast and lunchtime. (☑ 222 317 737; www.mistralcafe.cz; Valentinská 11; mains 80-290Kč; ⏰ 8am-11pm Mon-Fri, from 9am Sat & Sun; 🛜 👶; M Staroměstská)

Jewish Prague

Jews have been part of Prague for as long as it has existed, though their status has ebbed and flowed. For centuries, Jews were restricted to living in a small corner of the Old Town (today's Josefov). Some periods brought terror and pogroms, while others – the early 17th century – brought prosperity. In the 19th century, Jews were allowed to live outside their ghetto, but a century later most were murdered by the occupying Nazis.

Early Oppression

Jews began living in Prague in the 10th century, and by the 11th century the city was one of Europe's most important Jewish centres. The Crusades marked the start of the Jews' plight as the city's oldest synagogue was burned to the ground. By the end of the 12th century, they lost many rights; soon they were forced into a walled ghetto that was locked at night. For years Jews remained third-class citizens while emperors and the nobility argued over who should be in charge of Jewish affairs.

The Golden Age

The mid-16th to early-17th century is considered the golden age of Jewish history. Emperor Rudolf II (r 1576–1612) worked closely with Mayor Mordechai Maisel (1528–1601), at the time the wealthiest man in Prague. The community was led in spirit by noted mystic and Talmudic scholar Rabbi Loew (1525–1609).

Emancipation came in the 18th century under Habsburg Emperor Josef II. In 1848 Jews won the right of abode, meaning they could live where they wanted. The ghetto's walls were torn down and the Jewish quarter was renamed Josefov (to honour Josef II). As wealthy Jews moved out, the area slid into squalor. At the end of the 19th century, the area was levelled and rebuilt in art-nouveau splendour.

Destruction & Preservation

The Jewish community was largely destroyed by the Nazis in WWII, and only a few thousand Jews remain. One historic irony is that many of the Jewish Museum's holdings come from *shtetls* (Jewish villages) liquidated by the Nazis. Hitler had the artefacts brought here, chillingly, to build a 'museum of an extinct race'.

Drinking

Bokovka

WINE BAR

10 MAP P68, F2

Founded by a syndicate of oeno-
philes, including film directors
Jan Hřebejk and David Ondříček,
Bokovka has moved from its
original New Town location to this
hidden courtyard – look for the
red wine droplet sign; the door
is opposite it on the right. The
crumbling, atmospheric cellar
bar is a great place to sample the
best of Czech wines. The bar is
named after the movie *Sideways*
(*bokovka* in Czech), which was set
in Californian vineyards. (731 492
046; www.bokovka.com; Dlouhá 37;
5pm-1am Mon-Fri, from 3pm Sat;
6, 8, 15, 26)

Tretter's New York Bar

BAR

11 MAP P68, D3

This sultry 1930s Manhattan-style
cocktail bar harks back to swisher
times when people went out for
nightcaps – and when the drinks
were stiff and properly made.
Regularly rated as one of the
capital's top bars, Tretter's attracts
a stylish crowd and has prices to
match. Book your table in advance.
(224 811 165; www.tretters-bar.
cz; V Kolkovně 3; 7pm-3am; ;
Staroměstská)

Kozička

BAR

12 MAP P68, D3

Around for decades, the 'Little
Goat' is a buzzing, red-brick basement bar decorated with steel goat
sculptures, serving Krušovice on

Bokovka

VERONIKA PRIMM/LONELY PLANET ©

tap (50Kč for 500mL) and slightly pricey Czech pub food. It fills up later in the evening with a mostly studenty Czech crowd, and makes a civilised setting for a late-night session. (📞224 818 308; www.koz icka.cz; Kozí 1; ⏱6pm-4am Mon-Thu, to 5.30am Fri & Sat, 7pm-3am Sun; 📶; Ⓜ Staroměstská)

Entertainment

Dvořák Hall
CONCERT VENUE

13 ⭐ MAP P68, A3

The Dvořák Hall in the neo-Renaissance Rudolfinum (p71) is home to the world-renowned Czech Philharmonic Orchestra (Česká filharmonie). Sit back and be impressed by some of the best classical musicians in Prague. (Dvořákova síň; 📞227 059 227; www. ceskafilharmonie.cz; náměstí Jana Palacha 1, Rudolfinum; ⏱box office 10am-6pm Mon-Fri, to 3pm Jul & Aug; Ⓜ Staroměstská)

Roxy
LIVE MUSIC

14 ⭐ MAP P68, F2

Set in the ramshackle shell of an art-deco cinema, the legendary Roxy has nurtured the more independent end of Prague's club spectrum for almost three decades. This is the place to see Czechia's top DJs, and on the 1st floor is NoD, an 'experimental space' that stages drama, dance, cinema and live music. (📞608 060 745; www.roxy.cz; Dlouhá 33; tickets 150-800Kč; ⏱7pm-5am; 🚊6, 8, 15, 26)

Shopping

Gurmet Pasáž Dlouhá
FOOD & DRINKS

15 🔒 MAP P68, F2

Prague's foodie scene attains its apotheosis in this quite upmarket, art-deco arcade dedicated to fine food. As well as eateries such as **Naše Maso** (Our Meat; 📞222 311 378; http://nasemaso.ambi.cz; mains 75-195Kč; ⏱8.30am-10pm Mon-Sat; 📶) and **Banh Mi Makers** (📞732 966 621; www.facebook.com/banhmi makers; Hradební 1; mains 80-120Kč; ⏱11am-10pm Mon-Fri, noon-9pm Sat; 📶👪), you'll find shops selling Czech wines, artisanal cheeses, handmade chocolate and imported seafood. (Gourmet Arcade; Dlouhá 39; ⏱9am-10pm; 🚊6, 8, 15, 26)

Klára Nademlýnská
FASHION & ACCESSORIES

16 🔒 MAP P68, D3

Klára Nademlýnská is one of the country's top fashion designers, having trained in Prague and worked for almost a decade in Paris. Her clothes are characterised by clean lines, simple styling and quality materials, making for a very wearable range that covers the spectrum from swimwear to evening wear via jeans, halter tops, colourful blouses and sharply styled suits. (📞224 818 769; www. klaranademlynska.cz; Dlouhá 3; ⏱10am-7pm Mon-Fri, to 6pm Sat; Ⓜ Staroměstská)

Explore ◎
Old Town Square & Staré Město

Staré Město (Old Town), with its evocative medieval square, maze of alleyways, and quirky sights such as the Astronomical Clock, is the beating heart of the historic centre. Its origins date back to the 10th century, when a marketplace emerged on the Vltava's eastern bank. A thousand years later, it's as alive as ever, and surprisingly little changed by time.

The Short List

○ **Old Town Square (p78)** Prague's medieval centrepiece is a must-see for every visitor.

○ **Charles Bridge (p80)** Prague's 14th-century, Gothic bridge that spans the River Vltava with an open-air gallery of baroque statuary.

○ **Municipal House (p85)** One of Europe's most exuberant art-nouveau buildings containing highly decorative eateries, a concert hall and various salons.

○ **Astronomical Clock (p79)** The Old Town's medieval masterpiece puts on an automaton show on the hour, every hour.

○ **Estates Theatre (p94)** Grand old theatre where Mozart premiered Don Giovanni to an appreciative Prague audience.

Getting There & Around

🚊 Lines 2, 17 and 18 run to Staroměstská; lines 6, 8, 15 and 26 stop at Dlouhá třída.

Ⓜ Take line A to Staroměstská (the closest stop to Old Town Square) or line A or B to Můstek.

Neighbourhood Map on p84

Old Town Square (p78) LUCIANO MORTULA - LGM/SHUTTERSTOCK©

Top Experience

Gather in the Old Town Square

Laid with cobblestones and surrounded by spec-
tacular baroque churches, soaring spires, candy-
coloured buildings and a rococo palace, Old Town
Square is an architectural smorgasbord and a
photographer's delight. While the Astronomical
Clock – a mechanical marvel that still chimes on
the hour – is more than 600 years old, many of
the structures in the square are even older.

⊙ MAP P84, D1

Staroměstské náměstí

admission free

Ⓜ Staroměstská

Astronomical Clock

Built in 1490 by a master clockmaker named Hanuš, the **Astronomical Clock** (pictured) was a scientific feat in its day – even after various renovations, it remains a paradigm of antique technology. On the hour (from 9am to 9pm), crowds gather below for its quaint visual display.

Old Town Hall Clock Tower

Old Town Hall, dating from 1338, has more to offer than its clock. Climb (or take the lift) up the **clock tower** (Věž radnice; www.prague.eu; adult/child 250/150Kč; ⊘9am-10pm Tue-Sun, from 11am Mon; for privileged views over Old Town Square and the historic city centre.

Jan Hus Statue

Sitting near the centre of the square, Ladislav Šaloun's brooding art-nouveau statue of Jan Hus was unveiled on 6 July 1915, the 500th anniversary of Hus' death at the stake.

Church of Our Lady Before Týn

Straight out of a 15th-century fairy tale, the spiky, spooky Gothic spires of **Church of Our Lady Before Týn** (Kostel Panny Marie před Týnem; ☎222 318 186; www.tyn.cz; suggested donation 25Kč; ⊘10am-1pm & 3-5pm Mon-Sat, to noon Sun Mar-Dec, irregular hours Jan & Feb), aka Týn Church, are an unmistakable Old Town landmark. It also houses the tomb of Tycho Brahe.

Church of St Nicholas

This pretty baroque **monastery** (Kostel sv. Mikuláše; www.svmikulas.cz; admission free; ⊘10am-4pm Mon-Sat, noon-4pm Sun) is relatively new – finished in 1735, it replaced a Gothic church built here in the late 13th century. After several incarnations it now serves as a Czechoslovak Hussite church and a classical-concert venue.

★ Top Tips

o For the best views of the Astronomical Clock, come to the show at 9am or 10am. Arrive a few minutes before the hour.

o Look for lively food and craft stalls in Old Town Square around major holidays such as Christmas and Easter.

o Climb (or take the lift) up the clock tower for spectacular views over Old Town Square. Earlier is better.

o The most romantic time to visit the square is after dark, when the medieval buildings are beautifully illuminated.

✕ Take a Break

Enjoy a healthy meal at the vegetarian restaurant **Maitrea** (p91), just steps from the square. Otherwise there are countless touristy cafes on the square itself.

Top Experience

Walk Across Iconic Charles Bridge

You know a historic landmark is special when even the tourist crowds hardly dull its magnificence. So it is with Charles Bridge, Prague's signature monument. Commissioned in 1357, the massive, 520m-long stone bridge was the only link across the Vltava River between Prague Castle and the Old Town until 1741. It's particularly awe-inspiring at dawn in winter when fewest visitors are around.

◎ **MAP P84, A2**

Karlův most

🕐 24hr

🚋 2, 13, 14, 17, 18 to Karlovy lázně, 1, 5, 7, 12, 15, 20, 22, 25 to Malostranské náměstí

View from the Old Town Bridge Tower

Perched at the eastern end of Charles Bridge, the elegant late-14th-century **Old Town Bridge Tower** (Staroměstská mostecká věž; http://en.muzeumprahy.cz/prague-towers; adult/child 100/70Kč; ⏰10am-10pm Apr-Sep, to 8pm Mar & Oct, to 6pm Nov-Feb) was built not only as a fortification but also as a triumphal arch marking the entrance to the Old Town. Head upstairs for the dramatic view down over the crowded bridge.

Saintly Statues

The first monument erected on the bridge was the crucifix near the eastern end, in 1657. The first statue – the Jesuits' 1683 tribute to St John of Nepomuk – inspired other Catholic orders, and over the next 30 years a score more went up. Today most are copies, but a few of the originals can be seen at the Brick Gate & Casements at the Vyšehrad Citadel.

Rubbing St John of Nepomuk

The most famous statue is that of **St John of Nepomuk**, on the bridge's northern side, about halfway across. According to legend, Wenceslas IV had him thrown off the bridge in 1393 for refusing to divulge the queen's confessions (he was her priest). Tradition says that if you rub the bronze plaque, you will one day return to Prague.

Charles Bridge Museum

Examine the history of the Vltava's most famous crossing at the **Charles Bridge Museum** (Muzeum Karlova Mostu; www.charlesbridgemuseum.com; Křižovnické náměstí 3; adult/concession 170/70Kč; ⏰10am-6pm), located near the bridge's Old Town entrance. When you learn about the bridge's tumultuous 650-year history, including at least two perilous encounters with floods, you'll be surprised it's still standing.

★ Top Tips

o Visit the bridge at sunrise to beat the crowds.

o Keep your valuables close at hand: pickpockets lurk here, especially in summer.

o Plan to cross the bridge at least twice – once towards the castle and once away from it.

o Dawn is the ideal time for photos. In winter if it starts snowing, head for the bridge to capture some unforgettable images.

✗ Take a Break

Not far from the entrance to the Old Town side of the bridge, the student cafe **Café Kampus** (p93) is a great place to relax over a coffee or beer.

Splurge on a gourmet meal paired with Czech wine at **V Zátiší** (p90), close to the Old Town side of the bridge.

Walking Tour 🚶

Kafka's Prague

'This narrow circle encompasses my entire life', Franz Kafka (1883–1924) once said, drawing an outline around Prague's Old Town. While an exaggeration (he travelled and died abroad), Prague is a constant, unspoken presence in Kafka's writing, and this walk through the Old Town passes some of his regular haunts.

Start Náměstí Republiky;
Ⓜ Náměstí Republiky

End Hotel Intercontinental;
Ⓜ Staroměstská

Length 2km; 40 minutes

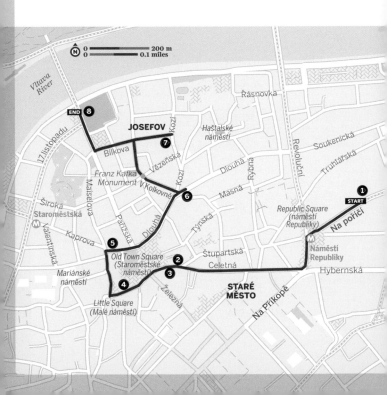

❶ Worker's Accident Insurance Company

Kafka's fiction was informed by his mundane day job as an insurance clerk – he worked for 14 years (1908–22) at the **Worker's Accident Insurance Company** at Na poříčí 7. His walk home passed the **Powder Gate** (p86) and the newly built **Municipal House** (p85).

❷ The House of the Three Kings

Just before Old Town Square, at Celetná 3, is the **House of the Three Kings**, where the Kafkas lived from 1896 to 1907. Franz's room, overlooking the **Church of Our Lady Before Týn** (p79), is where he wrote his first story.

❸ Sixt House

Across Celetná, the **Sixt House** was an earlier childhood home (1888–89). Nearby, at Staroměstské náměstí 17, is **At the Unicorn** (U Jednorožce) – home to Berta Fanta, who hosted literary salons for thinkers of the day, including Kafka and a young Albert Einstein.

❹ House of the Minute

The **House of the Minute** (dům U minuty), the Renaissance corner building attached to the Old Town Hall, was where Franz lived as a young boy (1889–96).

He later recalled being dragged to his school in Masná street by the family cook.

❺ Kafka's Birthplace

Just west of the **Church of St Nicholas** (p79) is **Kafka's birthplace**, marked by a bust of him at náměstí Franze Kafky 3 (formerly U Radnice 5). All that remains of the original house is the stone portal.

❻ Kafka's Bachelor Pad

Despite several fraught love affairs, Kafka never married and lived mostly with his parents. One of his few **bachelor flats** can be found at Dlouhá 16.

❼ Bílkova Apartment

Continuing north past the **Franz Kafka monument** (p71) you'll come to another of Kafka's temporary **apartments** at Bílkova 22. In 1914 he began *The Trial* here.

❽ Hotel Intercontinental

Head west to Pařížská and north towards the river. In the ground of the **Hotel Intercontinental** once stood another Kafka family apartment (1907–13), where Franz wrote his Oedipal short story 'The Judgment' (1912), and began *Metamorphosis*, about a man who transformed into a giant insect.

Old Town Square & Staré Město

For reviews see

⊙ Top Experiences	p78
⊙ Sights	p85
⊗ Eating	p90
⊗ Drinking	p91
⊕ Entertainment	p94
⊕ Shopping	p94

0 — 200 m
0 — 0.1 miles

Náměstí Republiky
U Obecního Domu
Municipal House 1
Powder Gate 3
15

Králodvorská
Rybná
Templová
Jakubská
Malá Štupartská
Štupartská

Na Příkopě
Nekázanka
Panská

Celetná
Myslbek pasáž
12

STARÉ MĚSTO

Haviřská

Former Fruit Market (Ovocný trh)
16

Železná
Open-Air Market
17

Kožná
9

Melantrichova
20
U Prince

Prague City Tourism

Týnská ulička
Týn Courtyard (Týnský dvůr)
Maitrea
22
21

Old Town Square & Astronomical Clock ⊙

Pařížská

Maiselova
Platnéřská
Linhartská
Žatecká

Little Square (Malé náměstí)
U Radnice

Prague City Tourism

Rytířská
Na Můstku
Mustek Ⓜ

Ryteřská
Provaznická
V kotcích

Wenceslas Square (Václavské náměstí)

Jungmannovo náměstí

Uhelný trh
6
Perlová

Michalská

Skořepka
Na Perštýně
Národní Třída Ⓜ

Jilská
Zlatá
18

V Kotcích
Havelská

Prague City Tourism

28. října
Mustek Ⓜ

Jungmannovo náměstí
Národní třída

Franciscan Garden (Františkánská zahrada)

Ⓜ Staroměstská

Alšovo nábřeží
Křižovnická

Valentinská
Kaprova
Mariánské náměstí
Husova
Seminářská

Klementinum
5

Charles Bridge ⊙

Křížovnické náměstí

Karlova
Liliová
Anenská
Retězová
Apple Museum
2
10
11

Náprstkova
14 8 13

Karoliny Světlé
Anenské náměstí

Bethlehem Chapel
4
7

Bethlehem Square (Betlémské náměstí)

Betlémská
Konviktská
Bartolomějská
Divadelní

19

Sights

Municipal House   HISTORIC BUILDING

1   MAP P84, F1

Prague's most exuberantly art-nouveau building is a labour of love, with every detail of its design and decoration carefully considered, and every painting and sculpture loaded with symbolism. The **restaurant** (☏222 002 770; www.francouzskarestaurace.cz; Náměstí Republiky 5; mains 425-735Kč; ⏰noon-11pm; 🛜; Ⓜ Náměstí Republiky) and cafe (p93) here are like walk-in museums of art-nouveau design, while upstairs there are half a dozen sumptuously decorated halls that you can visit by guided tour. You can look around the lobby and the downstairs bar for free, or book a guided tour in the information centre.

The Municipal House stands on the site of the Royal Court, seat of Bohemia's kings from 1383 to 1483 (when Vladislav II moved to Prague Castle), which was demolished at the end of the 19th century. Between 1906 and 1912 this magnificent art-nouveau edifice was built in its place – a lavish joint effort by around 30 leading artists of the day, creating a cultural centre that was the architectural climax of the Czech National Revival. The mosaic above the entrance, **Homage to Prague**, is set between sculptures representing the oppression and rebirth of the Czech people. Other sculptures ranged along the top of the facade represent history, literature, painting, music and architecture. You pass beneath a wrought-iron and stained-glass canopy into an interior that is art nouveau down to the doorknobs.First stop on the guided tour is the Smetana Hall (p94), Prague's biggest concert hall, with seating for 1200 beneath an art-nouveau glass dome. The stage is framed by sculptures representing the Vyšehrad legend (to the right) and Slavonic dances (to the left). On 28 October 1918 an independent Czechoslovak Republic was declared in the Smetana Hall, and in November 1989 meetings took place here between the Civic Forum and the Jakeš regime. The Prague Spring (p71) music festival always opens on 12 May, the day the Czech composer Smetana died, with a procession from Vyšehrad to the Municipal House followed by a gala performance of his symphonic cycle *Má vlast* (My Country) in the

Top Views of Old Town Square 🔭

The food might not be brilliant atop **U Prince** (Map p84, C2; ☏737 261 842; www.hoteluprince.com; Staroměstské náměstí 29; mains 269-649Kč; ⏰11am-11.30pm; Ⓜ Můstek), but the bird's-eye view of Old Town Square is unforgettable. Find its rooftop terrace by taking the lift at the back of the entrance hall to the top and climbing the stairs from there.

The Trials of Tycho Brahe

It's probably more than fair to describe Tycho Brahe, who's buried in the Church of Our Lady Before Týn (p79), as something of a character. This Danish father of modern astronomy catalogued thousands of stars, made stunningly accurate observations in an era before telescopes, and helped his assistant Johannes Kepler derive the laws of planetary motion.

He came to Prague in 1599 as Emperor Rudolf II's official mathematician. But Brahe also dabbled in astrology and alchemy. He lost part of his nose in a duel and wore a metal replacement. His pet moose apparently drank too much beer, fell down the stairs and died.

In Prague, Brahe himself died in 1601 of a bladder infection, reputedly because he was too polite to go to the toilet during a long banquet. Only recently have historians decided he was probably poisoned instead. We're not sure which version is more comforting.

Smetana Hall. Several impressive **official apartments** follow, but the highlight of the tour is the octagonal **Lord Mayor's Hall** (Primatorský sál), the windows of which overlook the main entrance. Every aspect of its decoration was designed by Alfons Mucha, who also painted the superbly moody murals that adorn the walls and ceiling. (Obecní dům; ☎ 222 002 101; www.obecnidum.cz; náměstí Republiky 5; guided tour adult/concession/child under 10yr 290/240Kč/free; ☉10am-8pm; Ⓜ Náměstí Republiky)

Apple Museum
MUSEUM

2 ◉ MAP P84, C2

This shrine to all things Apple claims to be the world's biggest private collection of Apple products, with at least one of everything made by the company between 1976 and 2012. Sleek white galleries showcase row upon row of crisply displayed computers, laptops, iPods and iPhones like sacred reliquaries. Highlights include the earliest Apple I and Apple II computers, an iPod 'family tree' and Steve Jobs' sneakers and jeans. There's also a section on Pixar films. (☎774 414 775; www.applemuseum.com; Husova 21; adult/child 240/100Kč; ☉10am-10pm; Ⓜ Staroměstská)

Powder Gate
TOWER

3 ◉ MAP P84, F1

Construction of the 65m-tall Powder Gate began in 1475 on the site of one of Staré Město's 13 original city gates. It remained unfinished until the great 19th-century neo-Gothicizer Jozef Mocker put the final touches to the building in

1886. The name comes from its use as a gunpowder magazine in the 18th century. The Gothic interior houses little more than a few information panels about the tower's construction – the main attraction is the view from the top. (Prašná brána; ☎725 847 875; http://en.muzeumprahy.cz/prague-towers; Na příkopě; adult/child 100/70Kč; �10am-10pm Apr-Sep, to 8pm Oct & Mar, to 6pm Nov-Feb; Ⓜ Náměstí Republiky)

Bethlehem Chapel CHURCH

4 ◉ MAP P84, B3

The Bethlehem Chapel is a national cultural monument, being the birthplace of the Hussite cause. Jan Hus preached here from 1402 to 1412, marking the emergence of the Reform movement from the sanctuary of the Karolinum (where he was rector). Every year on the night of 5 July, the eve of the anniversary of Hus's burning at the stake in 1415, a memorial is held here with speeches and bell-ringing. (Betlémská kaple; ☎224 248 595; www.bethlehemchapel.eu; Betlémské náměstí 3; adult/child 60/30Kč; �9am-6.30pm; ☐2, 13, 14, 17, 18)

Klementinum HISTORIC BUILDING

5 ◉ MAP P84, B2

The most overlooked of central Prague's attractions, the Klementinum is a vast complex of beautiful baroque and rococo halls, now mostly occupied by the Czech National Library. Most of the buildings are closed to the public, but you can walk freely

Municipal House (p85)

VARNAKOVR/SHUTTERSTOCK ©

The Astronomical Clock's Spectacle

Every hour on the hour, crowds gather beneath the Old Town Hall Tower to watch the Astronomical Clock in action. It's an amusing – if slightly underwhelming – performance that takes just under a minute to finish. Most people simply stand and gawk, but it's worth understanding a bit of the clock's historic (and highly photogenic) symbolism.

The four figures beside the clock represent the deepest civic anxieties of 15th-century Praguers: Vanity (with a mirror), Greed (with his telltale money bag), Death (the skeleton) and Pagan Invasion (represented by a Turk). The four figures below these are the Chronicler, Angel, Astronomer and Philosopher.

On the hour, Death rings a bell and inverts his hourglass, and the Twelve Apostles parade past the windows above the clock, nodding to the crowd. On the left side are Paul (with a sword and a book), Thomas (lance), Jude (book), Simon (saw), Bartholomew (book) and Barnabas (parchment); on the right side are Peter (with a key), Matthew (axe), John (snake), Andrew (cross), Philip (cross) and James (mallet). At the end, a cock crows and the hour is rung.

through the courtyards, or take a 50-minute **guided tour** of the baroque Library Hall, the Meridian Hall, the Astronomical Tower and (if no events are taking place) the Chapel of Mirrors.

When the Habsburg emperor Ferdinand I invited the Jesuits to Prague in 1556 to boost the power of the Roman Catholic Church in Bohemia, they selected one of the city's choicest pieces of real estate and in 1587 set to work on the **Church of the Holy Saviour** (kostel Nejsvětějšího Spasitele; www. farnostsalvator.cz; Křížovnické náměstí; admission free; ☺open for religious services), Prague's flagship of the Counter-Reformation. Its western facade faces Charles Bridge, with

its sooty stone saints glaring down at the traffic jam of trams and tourists on Křížovnické náměstí. After gradually buying up most of the adjacent neighbourhood, the Jesuits started building their college, the Klementinum, in 1653. By the time of its completion a century later it was the largest building in the city after Prague Castle. When the Jesuits fell out with the pope in 1773, it became part of Charles University. The baroque **Library Hall** (1727), magnificently decorated with ornate gilded carvings and a ceiling fresco depicting the Temple of Wisdom, houses thousands of theological volumes dating back to 1600. The **Meridian Hall** was used to determine the exact time of noon, using a beam of sunlight cast through a hole in one of the walls. Also dating from the 1720s, the 68m-tall **Astronomical Tower** is capped with a huge bronze of Atlas and was used as an observatory until the 1930s; it now houses a display of 18th-century astronomical instruments. The tower is still used today as Prague's weather station, with measurements taken without interruption since 1775, making it one of the longest-running series of weather reports in the world. The **Chapel of Mirrors** (Zrcadlová kaple) also dates from the 1720s and is an ornate confection of gilded stucco, marbled columns, fancy frescoes and ceiling mirrors – think baroque on steroids. Quality concerts of classical music are held here

daily (tickets are available at most ticket agencies). There are two other interesting churches in the Klementinum. The **Church of St Clement** (kostel sv Klimenta; Karlova; ⊙ services 8.30am & 10am Sun), lavishly redecorated in the baroque style from 1711 to 1715 to plans by Kilian Dientzenhofer, is now a Greek Catholic chapel. Conservatively dressed visitors are welcome to attend the services. And then there's the elliptical **Chapel of the Assumption of the Virgin Mary**, built in 1600 for the Italian artisans who worked on the Klementinum. (☏ 222 220 879; www.klementinum. com; entrances on Křížovnická, Karlova & Mariánské náměstí; guided tour adult/concession 300/200Kč; ⊙ 10am-6pm; Ⓜ Staroměstská, ⓠ 2, 17, 18)

Church of the Holy Saviour

Eating

U Dvou koček

CZECH €€

6 🍴 MAP P84, C4

A Prague classic, this traditional, been-here-forever beer hall and microbrewery, located under the arcading of Uhelný trh, is unmissable. The Urquell on tap is all well and good, but the restaurant's own Kočka lager better complements the hefty Bohemian fare on the menu. Every Czech knows this restaurant from its starring role in one of the best-known 1980s films, *Vrchní prchni!* (Waiter, Scarper!). (📞224 229 982; www.udvoukocek.cz; Uhelný trh 10; mains 199-399Kč; ⏱11am-11pm; 🛜; Ⓜ Můstek)

VERONIKA PRIMMJ/LONELY PLANET©

Lehká Hlava

V Zátiší

CZECH €€€

7 🍴 MAP P84, B3

Michelin-listed 'Still Life' is one of Prague's top restaurants, famed for the quality of its cuisine. The decor is bold and modern, with huge pieces of quirky glassware, boldly patterned wallpapers and cappuccino-coloured crushed-velvet chairs. The menu ranges from high-end Indian cuisine to gourmet versions of traditional Czech dishes – the South Bohemian goose in plum sauce is superb. (📞222 221 155; www.vzatisi.cz; Liliová 1; mains 595-745Kč; ⏱noon-3pm & 5.30-11pm; 🛜; 🚊2, 13, 14, 17, 18)

Lehká Hlava

VEGETARIAN €€

8 🍴 MAP P84, A3

Tucked away down a narrow cul-de-sac, the 'clear head' exists in a little world of its own. There are two exotically decorated dining rooms, both with a vaguely psychedelic vibe – tables lit from within, studded with glowing glass spheres or with a radiant wood-grain effect. In the kitchen the emphasis is on healthy, freshly prepared vegetarian and vegan dishes. (📞222 220 665; www.lehkahlava.cz; Boršov 2; mains 255-295Kč; ⏱11.30am-11.30pm Mon-Fri, noon-11.30pm Sat & Sun; 🖋👪; 🚊2, 17, 18)

Havelská Koruna

CAFETERIA €

 9 MAP P84, D2

For a taste of Slavic school-canteen fare that most Czechs eat on a daily basis, head to this self-service canteen north of Můstek. Pick up a *konzumační lístek* ('consumption chit') at the door, head to the serving counters where dinner ladies ladle out the staples of Bohemian and Moravian cuisine, eat at the communal benches and pay on the way out. You'll be in trouble if you lose that chit! Limited drinks (no coffee), separate counter for sweet mains and a clientele ranging from brave tourists to hungry office workers. (224 239 331; www.havelska-koruna.cz; Havelská 21; mains 50-150Kč; 10am-8pm; M Můstek)

Drinking

U Zlatého Tygra

PUB

 10 MAP P84, C2

Novelist Bohumil Hrabal's favourite tavern, the 'Golden Tiger' is one of the few Old Town drinking holes that has hung onto its soul – and its reasonable prices (48Kč per 450mL of Pilsner Urquell) – considering its location close to Old Town Square in a 14th-century townhouse. It's one of Prague's original pubs, but attracts few tourists. This is the place to which Václav Havel took Bill Clinton in 1994 to show him a real Czech pub. (222 221 111; www.uzlateho tygra.cz; Husova 17; 3-11pm; M Staroměstská)

Going Meatless in Staré Město

Prague's oldest quarter is home to several good vegetarian and vegan spots. Our favourites:

Country Life (Map p84, C2; 224 213 366; www.countrylife.cz; Melantrichova 15; per 100g 33-30Kč; 10.30am-7.30pm Mon-Thu, to 3.30pm Fri, noon-6pm Sun; M Můstek) All-vegan cafeteria offering inexpensive salads, vegetarian goulash, sunflower-seed burgers and soy drinks.

Lehká Hlava Down a narrow cul-de-sac, this simple, student-friendly spot exists in a little world of its own.

Maitrea (Map p84, D1; 774 422 226; www.restaurace-maitrea.cz; Týnská ulička 6; mains 235-270Kč; 11.30am-11.30pm, from noon Sat & Sun; M Staroměstská) Beautifully designed space with inventive vegetarian dishes.

Literary Prague

Prague has a well-deserved reputation as a literary heavyweight. The names Franz Kafka and Milan Kundera will be familiar to any serious reader, but Prague's writing roots run deeper – it's no accident the country's first postcommunist president, Václav Havel, was a playwright. In addition to its Czech writers, the city was also once a hotbed of German literature.

Czech Literary Lights

Besides the clever Kundera (b 1929), a staple on undergrad reading lists, Prague was home to humourist Bohumil Hrabal (1914–97), whose many books are widely translated into English. The film based on his novel *Closely Watched Trains* won the Oscar for Best Foreign Film in 1968. Another near-household name is Jaroslav Hašek (1883–1923), whose book *The Good Soldier Švejk* is a stroke of comic genius that recalls something of *Catch-22*. Czech poet Jaroslav Seifert won the Nobel Prize for poetry in 1984.

The German Connection

In the 19th and early 20th centuries, Prague was a centre of German literature. Kafka (1883–1924), a German-speaking Jewish writer, remains the gold standard: his books *The Trial* and *The Castle*, among many others, are modern classics. But Prague was also home to Kafka's friend and publisher Max Brod (1883–1924), as well as noted writers Egon Erwin Kisch (1885–1948) and Franz Werfel (1890–1945). One of the most beloved poets in the German language, Rainer Maria Rilke (1875–1926), was born and studied in Prague.

New Voices

There's no shortage of new Czech literary talent: Jáchym Topol (b 1962), Petra Hůlová (b 1979), Michal Viewegh (b 1962), Michal Ajvaz (b 1949), Emil Hakl (b 1958) and Miloš Urban (b 1967) are taking their places among the country's leading authors. They are pushing out old-guard figures such as Kundera, and are now seen as chroniclers of a very different, postcommunist age. Until recently, few books from these younger novelists had been translated into English. That's changing slowly as publishers appear more willing to take a chance on marketing them to English-speaking audiences.

U Tří Růží

BREWERY

11 🚇 MAP P84, C2

In the 19th century there were more than 20 breweries in Prague's Old Town, but by 1989 only one remained (U Medvídku). The Three Roses brewpub, on the site of one of those early breweries, helps revive the tradition, offering six beers on tap, including a tasty *světlý ležák* (pale lager; 56Kč per 400mL), good food and convivial surroundings. (📞601 588 281; www.u3r.cz; Husova 10; ⏱11am-11pm Sun-Thu, to midnight Fri & Sat; Ⓜ Staroměstská)

Kavárna Obecní Dům

CAFE

The spectacular cafe (see 15 ✳ Map p84, F1) in Prague's opulent Municipal House (p85) offers the opportunity to sip your cappuccino amid an orgy of art-nouveau splendour. In addition to the original decor, the cafe is known for its outstanding, Vienna-style gateaus. (📞222 002 763; www.kavarnaod.cz; náměstí Republiky 5, Municipal House; ⏱8am-11pm; 📶; Ⓜ Náměstí Republiky)

Grand Cafe Orient

CAFE

12 🚇 MAP P84, E2

There's food here, but most come to Prague's only cubist cafe to sip a brew as an excuse to admire the unique styling, which includes everything from teaspoons to lampshades. The Orient was designed by Josef Gočár in 1912

and was restored and reopened in 2005, having been closed since 1920. Decent coffee and inexpensive cocktails, but occasionally surly service. (📞224 224 240; www.grandcafeorient.cz; Ovocný trh 19; ⏱9am-10pm Mon-Fri, 10am-10pm Sat & Sun; Ⓜ Náměstí Republiky)

Café Kampus

CAFE

13 🚇 MAP P84, B3

This laid-back cafe doubles as an art gallery and event venue (talks, live music, lectures), and is hugely popular with students from Charles University. There are Czech newspapers and books to leaf through, chilled tunes on the sound system, and a long menu of gourmet teas, coffees and spirits. (📞775 755 143; www.cafekampus.cz; Náprstkova 10; ⏱10am-1am Mon-Fri, noon-1am Sat, noon-11pm Sun; 📶; 🚋2, 13, 14, 17, 18)

Hemingway Bar

COCKTAIL BAR

14 🚇 MAP P84, A3

The Hemingway is a snug and sophisticated hideaway with dark leather benches, a library-like back room, flickering candlelight, and polite and professional bartenders. There's a huge range of quality spirits (especially rum), first-class cocktails, champagne and cigars. (📞773 974 764; www.hemingwaybar.eu; Karolíny Světlé 26; ⏱5pm-1am Mon-Thu, to 2am Fri, 7pm-2am Sat, 7pm-1am Sun; 📶; 🚋2, 17, 18)

Entertainment

Smetana Hall CLASSICAL MUSIC

15 ⭐ MAP P84, F1

The unique Smetana Hall, centrepiece of the Municipal House (p85), is the city's largest concert hall, seating 1200 beneath an art-nouveau glass dome. The stage is framed by sculptures representing the Vyšehrad legend (right) and Slavonic dances (left). It's the home venue of the Prague Symphony Orchestra (Symfonický orchestr hlavního města Prahy; www.fok.cz), and stages music performances of all kinds. (Smetanova síň; ☎770 621 580; www.obecnidum.cz; Municipal House, náměstí Republiky 5; ⏱box office 10am-8pm; MNáměstí Republiky)

Estates Theatre OPERA

16 ⭐ MAP P84, D2

The Estates is the oldest theatre in Prague, with performances taking place uninterrupted since 1783, and famed as the place where Mozart conducted the premiere of *Don Giovanni* on 29 October 1787. This, and other Mozart operas, are regularly performed here, along with a range of classic opera, ballet and drama productions. (Stavovské divadlo; ☎224 902 322; www.narodni -divadlo.cz; Ovocný trh 1; ⏱box office 10am-6pm; MMůstek)

AghaRTA Jazz Centrum JAZZ

17 ⭐ MAP P84, D2

AghaRTA has been staging top-notch modern jazz, blues, funk and fusion since 1991, but moved into this central Old Town venue only in 2004. A typical jazz cellar with red-brick vaults, the centre also has a music shop (open 7pm to midnight) that sells CDs, T-shirts and coffee mugs. As well as hosting local musicians, AghaRTA occasionally stages gigs by leading international artists. (☎222 211 275; www.agharta.cz; Železná 16; cover 250Kč; ⏱7pm-1am, music 9pm-midnight; MMůstek)

Jazz Republic LIVE MUSIC

18 ⭐ MAP P84, C3

Despite the name, this relaxed club stages all kinds of live music, including rock, blues, reggae and fusion as well as jazz. Bands are mostly local, and the music is not overpowering – you can easily hold a conversation – which means it won't please the purists (sssshh!). (☎221 183 552; www.jazzrepublic.cz; Jilská 1a; admission free; ⏱8pm-late, music 9.15pm-midnight; MNárodní Třída)

Shopping

Kavka BOOKS

19 🅐 MAP P84, A4

Arguably the best place in Prague to pick up books on Czech art and photography you simply won't find anywhere else. It stocks everything from large-format coffee-table books to small prints covering every genre and artist the country has produced. Also has an e-shop and provides a shipping service. (☎606 030 202; www.kavkaartbooks.

com; cnr Krocínova & Karolíny Světlé; ⏰11am-7pm Mon-Fri, noon-5pm Sat; 🚊1, 2, 17, 18)

Modernista
HOMEWARES

Modernista (see **15** ⭐ Map p84, F1) specialises in reproduction 20th-century furniture, ceramics, glassware and jewellery in classic styles ranging from art deco and cubist to functionalist and Bauhaus. The main showroom with furniture is in **Vinohradský Pavilon** (Vinohradská tržnice; 🎫286 017 701; www.pavilon.cz; Vinohradská 50, Vinohrady; ⏰10am-7.30pm Mon-Fri, to 6pm Sat; Ⓜ Jiřího z Poděbrad, 🚊11, 13). This branch, located in the Municipal House information centre, is strong on jewellery and ceramics – items that might fit in your suitcase.(🎫222 002 102; www.modernista.cz; náměstí Republiky 5, Municipal House; ⏰10am-6pm; Ⓜ Náměstí Republiky)

Manufaktura
ARTS & CRAFTS

20 🔒 MAP P84, C2

There are seven of these kinds of Manufaktura outlets across town (another pared-down version has dozens of branches nationwide), but this small emporium near Old Town Square seems to keep its inventory especially enticing. You'll find great Czech wooden toys, beautiful-looking honey gingerbread made from elaborate medieval moulds, and seasonal gifts such as hand-painted Easter eggs.

(🎫601 310 611; www.manufaktura.cz; Melantrichova 17; ⏰10am-8pm; Ⓜ Můstek)

Botanicus
COSMETICS

21 🔒 MAP P84, E1

Around since the mid-90s, this now-international Czech chain produces natural health and beauty products made using herbs and plants grown on an organic farm at Ostrá, east of Prague. The scented soaps, herbal bath oils and shampoos, fruit cordials and handmade paper products make original souvenirs. Has branches in Český Krumlov and Karlovy Vary as well as 14 other countries. (🎫234 767 446; www.botanicus.cz; Týn 3; ⏰10am-6.30pm Nov-Mar, to 8pm Apr-Oct; Ⓜ Náměstí Republiky)

Bric A Brac
ANTIQUES

22 🔒 MAP P84, D1

This is a wonderfully cluttered cave of old household items, glassware, toys, apothecary jars, enamel signs, rusty bikes, typewriters and stringed instruments etc. Despite the junky look of the place, the knick-knacks (found in skips and attics across Bohemia) are shockingly expensive, but the affable Serbian owner can give you a guided tour around every piece in his extensive collection. (🎫222 326 484; Týnská 7; ⏰11am-6pm; Ⓜ Náměstí Republiky)

Old Town Square & Staré Město Shopping

Explore ◉

Wenceslas Square & Around

Busy Wenceslas Square, dating from 1348 and once a bustling horse market, was the site of several seminal events in Czech history. Today, it's crowded with souvenir shops, clubs, coffee chains and plenty of tourists, though it's possible to glimpse the square's previous grandeur simply by looking up at the glorious art-nouveau architecture.

The Short List

o **Wenceslas Square (p98)** *The country's largest square is the capital's commercial epicentre and often the backdrop to political protest.*

o **National Museum (p103)** *Newly renovated inside and out, this grand 19th-century museum is once again taking its rightful place as a top sight in Prague.*

o **Mucha Museum (p103)** *An entire museum dedicated to the life and works of the most famous of Prague artists.*

o **Museum of Communism (p103)** *Take a trip back in time to the stern and threadbare days of Czechoslovakia's communist regime.*

o **Prague State Opera (p108)** *The newly renovated opera is one of Central Europe's best.*

Getting There & Around

Ⓜ Lines A and B cross at Můstek at the bottom of the square. Lines A and C meet at Muzeum at the top.

Neighbourhood Map on p102

Adria Palace (p101) ISLAVICEK/SHUTTERSTOCK©

Top Experience 📷
Stroll along Buzzing Wenceslas Square

*This massive central square was founded by
Charles IV in 1348. For hundreds of years it was
called the 'Horse Market' and featured a small
lake, horse-drawn trams and the first Czech theatre. On 28 October 1918, the independent republic
of Czechoslovakia was announced here; in 1945
the end of WWII was declared and celebrated.
Later, during the Velvet Revolution, the square
hosted huge, historic demonstrations.*

👁 MAP P102, C3

Václavské náměstí

Ⓜ Můstek, Muzeum

Jan Palach Memorial

In January 1969 university student Jan Palach set fire to himself in front of the National Museum to protest against the Soviet-led invasion of Czechoslovakia the preceding August. Palach later died from his wounds and became a national hero. The **memorial** sits at the exact spot where Palach fell, marked by a cross in the pavement just below the steps to the museum's entrance.

Former Radio Free Europe Building

During the Cold War, many Czechs and Slovaks turned to US-financed Radio Free Europe for news from the West. After 1989 the radio moved its headquarters from Munich to the former Czechoslovak Federal Parliament building (at the top of the square, just to the left of the National Museum). In 2008 RFE moved to a new building in the Prague suburbs, and the **old headquarters** (www.nm.cz; Vinohradská 1; adult/child 200/130Kč; ◷10am-6pm) is now used as a National Museum annex.

St Wenceslas Statue

The focal point of Wenceslas Square is the **equestrian statue of St Wenceslas** (pictured) at its southern end. Sculptor Josef Myslbek has surrounded the 10th-century Duke of Bohemia (and 'Good King Wenceslas' of Christmas-carol fame) with four other patron saints of Bohemia – Prokop, Adalbert, Agnes and Ludmila.

Grand Hotel Evropa

Grand indeed – this ornate **art-nouveau hotel** and cafe is easily the most colourful building on a colourful square. Unfortunately it was closed for renovation at the time of research and it's not clear when it will reopen.

★ Top Tips

o During holidays and festivals, try the square's food and drink stands for local specialities such as spiced wine and grilled sausage.

o Keep an eye on your belongings, especially at night – this area is notorious for pickpockets and touts.

o Many restaurants on the square are tourist traps; better-value options are nearby.

✕ Take a Break

Within the Lucerna shopping arcade on Wenceslas Square's southern side (enter from either Vodičkova or Štěpánská), the elegant, 1920s-style **Kavárna Lucerna** (☏224 215 495; www.restaurace-monarchie.cz/en/cafe-lucerna; Pasáž Lucerna, Štěpánská 61; ◷10am-midnight; ☎; ◫3, 5, 6, 9, 14, 24) is a great place for a quick coffee.

Walking Tour 🥾

Velvet Revolution

It's been more than 30 years since 1989's Velvet Revolution, when Czechs peacefully overthrew their communist overlords, but it will always be a landmark event. This walk takes you past the sites of the large-scale protests, strikes and press conferences that heralded epic change in the country.

Start Národní třída;
Ⓜ Národní třída

End Former Radio Free Europe Building;
Ⓜ Muzeum

Length 2km; 45 minutes

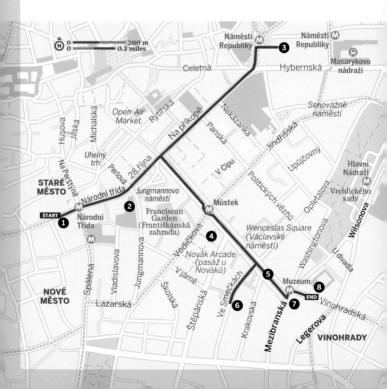

❶ Student Memorial

Start where the revolution itself began. The **bronze sculpture** on the side of a lawyer's office marks the tragic events of 17 November 1989, when tens of thousands of students marching to remember Czechs murdered in WWII were attacked by riot police.

❷ Adria Palace

The beautiful, rondocubist **Adria Palace** temporarily served as the headquarters of Civic Forum, the umbrella group formed by Václav Havel to represent the protesters and their demands. In the weeks after 17 November, this was a beehive of dissident activity.

❸ Museum of Communism

The **Museum of Communism** (p103) illuminates local communist history – and the lies, privations and humiliations that ultimately drove the revolution demanding the regime's end. A short, graphic film shows the events of 1989.

❹ Melantrich Building

The action soon spread to nearby Wenceslas Square and the **Melantrich Building**, now a Marks & Spencer. On 24 November, Havel and deposed 'Prague Spring' president Alexander Dubček addressed the crowds from its balcony.

❺ St Wenceslas Statue

The **Wenceslas Statue** (p99), at the upper end of the square, was bedecked by protesters with flags, posters and political slogans.

❻ Činoherní Klub Theatre

Prague's theatres were used for public discussions. The Civic Forum was formed on 19 November at **Činoherní Klub Theatre** (Ve Smečkách 26) and immediately demanded the resignations of communist functionaries.

❼ Jan Palach Memorial

Just in front of the **National Museum** is the **Jan Palach Memorial** (p99), an inlaid cross for a student who set himself on fire in 1969 to protest the Soviet-led Warsaw Pact invasion of the previous year – becoming a national hero in the process.

❽ Former Radio Free Europe Building

At the top of the square, left of the National Museum, stands the former **building** (p99) for Radio Free Europe, the US-funded radio station that helped bring down the communist regime. It now houses a branch of the National Museum.

Wenceslas Square & Around

For reviews see
- ◆ Top Experiences p98
- ◎ Sights p103
- ✕ Eating p104
- ✕ Drinking p107
- ✪ Entertainment p108
- ⊞ Shopping p109

1 National Museum
2 Mucha Museum
3 ◎
4 Hotel Jalta Nuclear Bunker
5 Church of Our Lady of the Snows

Praha hlavní nádraží (Main Train Station)

Hlavní Nádraží

Vrchlického sady

Wilsonova

Senovážné náměstí

Jindřišská

Senovážná

Jeruzalémská

Opletalova

Washingtonova

Růžová

Lupáčova

Politických vězňů

U divadla

Legerova

Vinohradská

Mezibranská

Muzeum

Krakovská

Ve Smečkách

Štěpánská

Washingtonova

Nekázanka

Panská

V cípu

Jindřišská

Na Příkopě

Havířská

Provaznická

Rytířská

Na Můstku

Můstek

Mucha Museum

Wenceslas Square

Novák Arcade (pasáž u Nováků)

V Jámě

Vodičkova

Franciscan Garden (Františkánská zahrada)

Jungmannovo náměstí

28. října

Perlová

Uhelný trh

Národní třída

Národní Třída

Jungmannova

Palackého

Lazarská

Vladislavova

Purkyňova

Spálená

Školská

Cafe Louvre

Španělská

Balbínova

Polská

Mánesova

0   200 m
0   0.1 miles

Sights

National Museum MUSEUM

1 MAP P102, D4

Looming above Wenceslas Square is the neo-Renaissance bulk of the National Museum, designed in the 1880s by Josef Schulz as an architectural symbol of the Czech National Revival. Its magnificent interior is a shrine to the cultural, intellectual and scientific history of Czechia. The museum's main building reopened in 2018 after several years of renovation work, but the permanent exhibition is yet to be reinstalled. (Národní muzeum; ☎224 497 111; www. nm.cz; Václavské náměstí 68; adult/child 200/130Kč; ☺10am-6pm; MMuzeum)

Mucha Museum GALLERY

2 MAP P102, C1

This fascinating, busy but overpriced museum features the sensuous art-nouveau posters, paintings and decorative panels of Alfons Mucha (1860–1939), as well as many sketches, photographs and other memorabilia. The exhibits include countless artworks showing Mucha's trademark Slavic maidens with flowing hair and piercing blue eyes, bearing symbolic garlands and linden boughs.

There are also photos of the artist's Paris studio, one of which shows a trouserless Gaugin playing the harmonium; a powerful canvas entitled *Old Woman in Winter;* and the original of the 1894 poster of actress Sarah Bernhardt as Giselda, which shot him to international fame. In 1910 Mucha was invited to design the Lord Mayor's Hall in Prague's Municipal House (p85), and following the creation of Czechoslovakia in 1918, he designed the new nation's banknotes and postage stamps.The fascinating video documentary about Mucha's life is well worth watching, and helps put his achievements in perspective. (Muchovo muzeum; ☎224 216 415; www.mucha.cz; Panská 7; adult/child 300/200Kč; ☺10am-6pm; ☐3, 5, 6, 9, 14, 24)

Museum of Communism MUSEUM

3 MAP P102, D1

Put together by an American expat and his Czech partner, Prague's priciest private museum tells the story of Czechoslovakia's years behind the Iron Curtain in photos, words and a fascinating and varied collection of...well, stuff. (Muzeum Komunismu; ☎224 212 966; www. muzeumkomunismu.cz; V Celnici 4; adult/concession 380/290Kč; ☺9am-8pm; MMůstek)

Hotel Jalta Nuclear Bunker HISTORIC BUILDING

4 MAP P102, D3

Hidden beneath the 1950s Hotel Jalta on Wenceslas Square lies a communist-era nuclear shelter that was opened to the public in 2013. The tour, led by a guide in period security-police uniform, takes in a series of secret

Much Ado About Mucha

Alfons Mucha (1860–1939) is the Czech answer to Austria's Gustav Klimt, England's William Morris, or Scotland's Charles Rennie Mackintosh.

One of the fathers – if not *the* father – of art nouveau as represented in the visual arts, he first found fame in Paris after producing a stunning poster for actress Sarah Bernhardt's 1895 play *Gismonda*. A contract with Bernhardt, reams of advertising work and trips to America brought him international renown.

Mucha returned home in 1909, and went on to design the banknotes for the first Czechoslovak Republic after 1918. Around this time, he also produced his opus, a collection of 20 gigantic canvases telling the history of the Slavic peoples, which he titled the *Slav Epic (Slovanská epopej)*.

Mucha created some of the stunning interiors of Prague's Municipal House (p85) and designed a beautiful stained-glass window for St Vitus Cathedral (p38). His signature art-nouveau work is on display at the Mucha Museum (p103).

chambers. The highlight is the communications room, where wiretaps in the bedrooms of important guests were monitored. (The Cold War Museum Crisis fallout shelter; http://en.muzeum-studene-valky.cz/vstupne; Václavské náměstí 45; adult/child 200/130Kč; ⏱tours in English 1pm, 2.30pm, 4pm & 5.30pm; Ⓜ Muzeum)

Church of Our Lady of the Snows

CHURCH

5 ◉ MAP P102, B2

This Gothic church at the northern end of Wenceslas Square was begun in the 14th century by Charles IV, but only the chancel was ever completed, which accounts for its proportions – seemingly taller than it is long. Charles had intended it to be the largest church in Prague, but the Hussite wars brought work to an end. The nave is higher than that of St Vitus Cathedral, and the altar is the city's tallest. (Kostel Panny Marie Sněžné; www.pms.ofm.cz; Jungmannovo náměstí 18; ⏱7am-7pm; Ⓜ Můstek)

Eating

Cukrárna Myšák

CAFE $

6 ✖ MAP P102, B3

Opened by confectioner František Myšák in 1911 and redesigned by artist Josef Čapek (brother of Karel) in 1922, the Myšák has had a long and turbulent history, but has survived to this day as a classic Prague *cukrárna* (cafe bakery), albeit a pricey one in its current incarnation. Top-notch cakes and coffee, a super-central location and an illustrious past make this a must-visit. (📞730 589 249; www.mysak.ambi.cz; Vodičkova 31; cakes from 45Kč; ⏰7.30am-7pm Mon-Fri, from 9am Sat & Sun; 🚋3, 5, 6, 9, 14, 24)

Dhaba Beas VEGETARIAN $

7 🍴 MAP P102, C3

Dhaba Beas vegetarian self-service restaurants have been around in obscure parts of Prague for years, but this new, clean-cut version within the Lucerna Passage is in an easily findable location and offers a stable selection of tasty salads, spicy mains and healthy drinks. A bit of respite from pig knuckle, even for devoted carnivores. (www.dhababeas.cz; Štěpánská 61, Pasáž Lucerna; per 100g 22.90Kč; ⏰11am-9pm Mon-Fri, noon-8pm Sat & Sun; 🛜🖉; 🚋3, 5, 6, 9, 14, 24)

Výtopna CZECH $$

8 🍴 MAP P102, D4

Got a soft spot for choo-choos, or have the kids had enough of Charles IV and Jan Hus? Then head for this gimmicky restaurant concept right on Wenceslas Square, where drinks can be delivered to guests' tables by model trains on long tracks. While the beer is reasonably priced, the food is pricey, but there is a kids' menu. If you reserve online, make sure the staff know you want a table served by train. (📞775 444 554; https://vytopna.cz/pages/vaclavak; Václavské náměstí 56; mains 239-399Kč; ⏰11am-midnight; 🛜🚻; Ⓜ Muzeum)

National Museum (p103)

Oppression & Revolution

From Coup to Invasion

February 1948 marked the start of a half-century's worth of political turmoil in Prague. It was at this time that the leaders of the Czechoslovak Communist Party (KSČ), not content with a controlling position in the postwar coalition after the 1946 elections, staged a coup d'état backed by the Soviet Union. The next two decades saw widespread political persecution.

In the late 1960s, Communist Party leader Alexander Dubček loosened the reins slightly under the banner 'Socialism With a Human Face'. There was a resurgence in literature, theatre and film, led by the likes of Milan Kundera, Bohumil Hrabal, Václav Havel and Miloš Forman. The Soviet regime crushed this 'Prague Spring' on 20 and 21 August 1968, using Warsaw Pact tanks, and Dubček was replaced by hardliner Gustáv Husák.

The Fall of Communism

The Husák government expelled many reform communists from positions of authority and introduced what Czechs called 'normalisation' – in other words, Soviet-style repression. Active dissent was limited to a few hundred people, mostly intellectuals and artists, including playwright Havel.

In November 1989, as communist regimes tumbled across Eastern Europe, the Czechoslovak government came under increasing pressure to relinquish power. On 17 November riot police cracked down on a peaceful student protest march, which would prove to be the catalyst to revolution. Within days, crowds on Wenceslas Square swelled to some 500,000 people.

A group led by Havel procured the government's resignation on 3 December, and 26 days later, he was the new leader. The 'Velvet Revolution', named for its peaceful nature (as well as the inspiration its leaders took from the rock band the Velvet Underground), had triumphed.

A Velvet Divorce

The transition to democracy was anything but smooth, though it eventually succeeded. One casualty of the revolution was the splitting of the country into separate Czech and Slovak states in 1993. The amicable break up later became known as the 'Velvet Divorce'.

Drinking

Vinograf   WINE BAR

9 🟢 MAP P102, E1

With knowledgeable staff, a relaxed atmosphere and an off-the-beaten-track feel, this appealingly modern wine bar is a great place to discover Moravian wines. There's good finger food – mostly cheese and charcuterie – to accompany your wine, with food and wine menus (in Czech and English) on big blackboards behind the bar. Very busy at weekends, when it's worth booking a table. There's another popular branch in **Malá Strana** (📞604 705 730; Míšeňská 8; ⏱4pm-midnight Mon-Sat, 2-10pm Sun; 📶; 🚋12, 15, 20, 22, 23). (📞214 214 681; www.vinograf.cz; Senovážné náměstí 23; ⏱11.30am-midnight Mon-Fri, from 5pm Sat; 📶; 🚋3, 5, 6, 9, 14, 24)

Hoffa   COCKTAIL BAR

10 🟢 MAP P102, E1

Low-lit design is the key feature here – a long (12m!) bar fronting a big space with sleek, functional decor and a wall of windows looking out onto Senovážné náměstí's fountain of dancing sprites. Friendly staff, accomplished cocktails and good food – you'll struggle to find a table at lunchtime. (📞601 359 659; www.hoffa.cz; Senovážné náměstí 22; ⏱11am-2am Mon-Fri, 6pm-2am Sat, 6pm-midnight Sun; 📶; 🚋3, 5, 6, 9, 14, 24)

Hoffa

Entertainment

Lucerna Music Bar   LIVE MUSIC

11 ⭐ MAP P102, C3

Nostalgia reigns supreme at this atmospheric old theatre, now looking a little dog-eared. It hosts all kinds of acts – from Czech superstars to amateur strummers from all over the country – plus there's a hugely popular 1980s and '90s video party from 9pm every Friday and Saturday night, with crowds of often not-so-young locals bopping along to Depeche Mode and Modern Talking. (📞224 217 108; www.musicbar.cz; Palác Lucerna, Vodičkova 36; 🕤9.30am-1am Mon-Sat; Ⓜ Můstek)

Prague State Opera   OPERA

12 ⭐ MAP P102, E3

The impressive neo-rococo home of the Prague State Opera provides a glorious setting for performances of opera and ballet. (Státní opera Praha; 📞224 901 448; www.narodni-divadlo.cz; Wilsonova 4; 🕤box office 10am-6pm; Ⓜ Muzeum)

Kino Světozor   CINEMA

13 ⭐ MAP P102, C3

The Světozor is under the same management as Žižkov's famous **Kino Aero** (📞271 771 349; www.kinoaero.cz; Biskupcova 31, Žižkov; tickets 60-120Kč; 📶; 🚋1, 9, 10, 11, 16), but is more central, and has the same emphasis on classic cinema, documentary and art-house films screened in their original language – everything from *Battleship Potemkin* and *Casablanca* to *Annie Hall* and *The Motorcycle Diaries* – plus critically acclaimed box office hits. (📞224 946 824; www.kinosvetozor.cz; Vodičkova 41; tickets 70-145Kč; 📶; Ⓜ Můstek)

Shopping 'At the Moat'

Crossing the lower end of Wenceslas Square, Na Příkopě is one of the city's prettiest and most popular promenades. The name translates as 'At the Moat' – the street traces a moat that once ran between Staré Město and Nové Město to protect the Old Town from attack.

In the 19th century, Na Příkopě was the fashionable haunt of Austrian cafe society. Today it's typical high-street shopping turf, lined with international retail chains such as H&M and Mango and Zara, and dotted with colourful shopping malls, including dům U černé růže (House of the Black Rose) at No 12, Myslbek pasáž (www.myslbek.com) at No 21, Slovanksý dům at No 22, and Palladium (www.palladiumpraha.cz) at náměstí Republiky 1.

Shopping

Baťa
SHOES

14 🔒 MAP P102, B2

Established by Tomáš Baťa in 1894, the Baťa footwear empire is still in family hands and is one of Czechia's most successful companies. The flagship store on Wenceslas Square, built in the 1920s, is considered a masterpiece of modern architecture, and houses six floors of shoes (including international brands as well as Baťa's own), handbags, luggage and leather goods. (📞221 088 478; www.bata.cz; Václavské náměstí 6; ⏰9am-9pm Mon-Sat, 10am-9pm Sun; Ⓜ Můstek)

Moser
GLASS

15 🔒 MAP P102, C1

The most exclusive and respected of Bohemian glassmakers, Moser was founded in Karlovy Vary in 1857 and is famous for its rich and flamboyant designs. The shop on Na Příkopě is probably more for browsing than for the glass (even small items cost thousands of crowns) as it's in a magnificently decorated, originally Gothic building called the House of the Black Rose *(dům U černé růže)*. (📞224 211 293; www.moser-glass.com; Na Příkopě 12; ⏰10am-8pm Mon-Fri, to 7pm Sat & Sun; Ⓜ Můstek)

Explore ⊕
Nové Město

Nové Město is a long, arching neighbourhood that borders Staré Město on its eastern and southern edges. The name translates as 'New Town', which is something of a misnomer since the area was established nearly 700 years ago by Emperor Charles IV. But unlike Staré Město or Malá Strana, the historic feeling is missing here, owing mainly to massive reconstruction in the 19th century.

The Short List

○ **National Theatre (p118)** *Built in the late 19th century with donations from around the Czech lands, this remains the country's top stage.*

○ **Kavárna Slavia (p116)** *The country's most famous cafe is a hangout for actors, writers and curious tourists.*

○ **Náplavka Farmers Market (p119)** *The capital's top outdoor market takes place by the sluggish waters of the Vltava.*

○ **Reduta Jazz Club (p118)** *Prague's premier jazz joint can compete with any in the world.*

○ **U Fleků (p117)** *The best-known of Prague's beer halls has been brewing beer for at least 500 years.*

Getting There & Around

🚃 2, 9, 18, 22, 23 to Národní třída.

Ⓜ Line B to Můstek or Karlovo Náměstí; Line A to Můstek.

Neighbourhood Map on p112

National Theatre (p118) BTWCAPTURE/500PX©

For reviews see

◉ Sights	p113
✕ Eating	p115
✕ Drinking	p116
✕ Entertainment	p118
🛍 Shopping	p119

200 m
0.1 miles

Mezibranská

Muzeum Ⓜ

Czech
Blind
United

Krakovská

Wenceslas
Square
(Václavské
náměstí)

Ve Smečkách

Štěpánská

Mústek Ⓜ

8 ✕

Franciscan Garden
(Františkánska
zahrada)

Lucerna Palace
(Palác Lucerna)

Vodičkova

Palackého

Vejnarna

Na Rybníčku II.

Ječná

19 🛍

Lipová

Kateřinská

IP Pavlova Ⓜ

Školská

Řezníčka

Navrátilova

Žitná

Mústek Ⓜ

Adria
Palace

K (David
Černý Sculpture)

Jungmannova

5 ◉

Národní
Třída

Purkyňova

Vladislavova

Lazarská

Malá Štěpánská

Charles Square
(Karlovo
náměstí)

4 ◉ Charles Square

Vyšehradská

13 🛍

Spálená

Ⓜ

16 ✕ 10

18

Na Perštýně

Mikulandská

Václav Havel
Library

Ostrovní

2 ◉

Černá

NOVÉ
MĚSTO

14 ◉

Spálená

Karlovo
Náměstí

Odborů

Bartolomějská

V Jirchářích

Vorsilská

Opatovická

12 🛍

Kremencová

6 ✕

Myslíkova

Na Zderaze

National Memorial to
the Heroes of the
Heydrich Terror

Václavská

17 🛍

Divadelní

Národní třída

Pštrossova

Nástruže

Vojtěšská

7 ✕

Šítkov

Václavská

Dittrichova

Resslova

20 🛍

Jirásek
Square
(Jiráskovo
náměstí)

Jiráskův
Bridge
(Jiráskův
most)

Smetanovo nábřeží

15 🛍 11

Masarykovo nábřeží

9 ✕

Slav Island
(Slovanský
ostrov)

Sights

Prague City Museum   MUSEUM

1 ◎ MAP P112, F2

This excellent, oft-overlooked museum, opened in 1898, is devoted to the history of Prague from prehistoric times to the 20th century (labels are in English as well as Czech). Among the many intriguing exhibits are an astonishing scale model of Prague, and the Astronomical Clock's original 1866 calendar wheel with Josef Mánes' beautiful painted panels representing the months – that's January at the top, toasting his toes by the fire, and August near the bottom, sickle in hand, harvesting the corn. (Muzeum hlavního města Prahy; ☏221 709 674; www.muzeumprahy.cz; Na poříčí 52; adult/child 150/60Kč; ⏰9am-6pm Tue-Sun; Ⓜ Florenc)

Václav Havel Library   LIBRARY

2 ◎ MAP P112, B2

This small exhibition and library, supported by the foundation that protects the legacy of the late playwright-president, houses a permanent exhibition on the life and work of Václav Havel called *Havel in a Nutshell* (*Havel v Kostce* in Czech), which includes fascinating photos from throughout the ex-president's life, quotations and touch screens.

An English tour of the library can be arranged by emailing ahead (info@vaclavhavel-library.org). The archives are open for researchers every Tuesday from 9am until 5pm. (Knihovna Václava Havla; ☏222 220 112; www.vaclavhavel-library.org; Ostrovní 13; admission free; ⏰noon-5pm Tue-Sat; 🚋1, 2, 9, 13, 14, 17, 18, 22, 23)

Prague Main Train Station   ARCHITECTURE

3 ◎ MAP P112, F2

What, a railway station as a tourist attraction? Perhaps not all of it, but it's certainly worth heading to the top floor for a look at the newly renovated splendour of the original art-nouveau entrance hall, designed by Josef Fanta and built between 1901 and 1909.

The domed interior is adorned with a mosaic of two nubile ladies, the Latin inscription *Praga: mater urbium* (Prague: Mother of Cities) and the date '28.*října* r:1918' (28 October 1918, Czechoslovakia's Independence Day). The hall, which once served as the main ticket office (you can still see the ticket windows), now houses a cafe. (Praha hlavní nádraží; Wilsonova; ⏰3.15am-12.40am; Ⓜ Hlavní Nádraží)

Charles Square   SQUARE

4 ◎ MAP P112, C4

With an area of more than seven hectares, Charles Square is Prague's biggest – it's more like a small park, really, and was originally the city's cattle market. Presiding over it is the **Church of St Ignatius** (kostel sv Ignáce; Ječná 2; Ⓜ Karlovo Náměstí), a 1660s baroque tour de force designed for the Jesuits by Carlo Lurago. The

Heroic Paratroopers

In 1941, during WWII, the occupying Nazi government appointed SS general Reinhard Heydrich, Hitler's heir apparent, as Reichsprotektor of Bohemia and Moravia. The move came in response to a series of crippling strikes and sabotage operations by the Czech resistance movement, and Heydrich immediately cracked down with a vengeance.

In an effort to support the resistance and boost Czech morale, Britain secretly trained a team of Czechoslovak paratroopers to assassinate Heydrich. The daring mission was code-named 'Operation Anthropoid' – and against all odds it succeeded. On 27 May 1942, two paratroopers, Jan Kubiš and Jozef Gabčík, attacked Heydrich as he rode in his official car through the city's Libeň district; he later died from the wounds.

The assassins and five co-conspirators fled but were betrayed in their hiding place in the Church of Sts Cyril & Methodius; all seven died in the ensuing siege. This moving story is told at the **National Memorial to the Heroes of the Heydrich Terror** (Národní památník hrdinů Heydrichiády; Map p112, B4; 222 540 718; www.vhu.cz/muzea/ostatni-expozice/krypta; Resslova 9a; admission free; ⏰9am-5pm Tue-Sun; Ⓜ Karlovo Náměstí), located at the church.

The Nazis reacted with a frenzied wave of terror, which included the annihilation of two entire Czech villages, Ležáky and Lidice, and the shattering of the underground movement.

rather scruffy piazza outside is due to undergo thorough gentrification in coming years.

The baroque palace at the southern end of the square belongs to Charles University. It's known as **Faust House** (Faustův dům; Karlovo náměstí 40; Ⓜ Karlovo Náměstí) because, according to a popular German legend, this was where Mephistopheles took Dr Faust away to hell through a hole in the ceiling. The building also has associations with Rudolf II's English court alchemist, Edward Kelley, who toiled here in the 16th century trying to convert lead into gold. (Ⓜ Karlovo Náměstí)

K (David Černý Sculpture)

PUBLIC ART

5 ◎ MAP P112, C1

Located in the courtyard of the up-market Quadrio shopping centre above Národní třída metro station, David Černý's giant rotating bust of Franz Kafka is formed from 39 tonnes of mirrored stainless steel. It's a mesmerising show as Kafka's face rhythmically dissolves and re-emerges, possibly playing on notions of the author's ever-changing personality and sense of self-doubt. Many stand for ages watching the spectacle. (Statue of Kafka; Quadrio, Spálená 22; admission free; [M]Národní Třída)

Eating

Globe Bookstore & Café
CAFE €

6 [X] MAP P112, B3

This appealing expat bookshop-cafe serves nachos, burgers, chicken wings and salads until 11pm (to 10pm Sunday), and also offers an excellent brunch menu (9.30am to 3pm Saturday and Sunday) that includes an American classic (bacon, egg and hash browns), full English fry-up, blueberry pancakes and freshly squeezed juices. Lighter breakfasts are served from 10am to noon weekdays. ([J]224 934 203; www.globebookstore.cz; Pštrossova 6; mains 150-300Kč; [⊙]10am-11pm Mon-Fri, 9.30am-12.30am Sat, 9.30am-10.30 Sun; [�]; [M]Karlovo Náměstí)

Klub Cestovatelů
MIDDLE EASTERN €€

7 [X] MAP P112, A3

Run by travel enthusiasts, this Lebanese restaurant and tearoom cultivates a relaxed and welcoming atmosphere, with its wicker chairs, knick-knacks and library of travel guidebooks. End a meal of baba ganoush, falafel, hummus or lamb kebabs with some authentic Middle Eastern desserts and a speciality tea. Also hosts countless travel-related events that are not

K: The Head of Franz Kafka by David Černý

MARBEN/SHUTTERSTOCK©

Nové Město Eating

always in Czech. The cheap lunch menu (109Kč to 129Kč) is a steal. (📞734 322 729; www.klubcestovatelu. cz; Masarykovo nábřeží 22; mains 69-300Kč; ⏰11am-11pm Mon-Fri, noon-11pm Sat, noon-10pm Sun; 📶🚭♿; 🚊17)

Café Imperial INTERNATIONAL €€

8 🍴 MAP P112, E1

First opened in 1914, and given a complete facelift in 2007, the Imperial is a tour de force of art-nouveau tiling – the walls and ceiling are covered in original ceramic tiles, mosaics, sculptured panels and bas-reliefs, with period light fittings and bronzes scattered about. The menu ranges from American breakfasts to Czech classics to roast quail. Best for a relatively inexpensive but stylish start to the day. (📞246 011 440; www.cafeimperial.cz; Na poříčí 15; mains 165-455Kč; ⏰7am-11pm; 📶; Ⓜ Náměstí Republiky)

Art Restaurant Mánes FRENCH €€

9 🍴 MAP P112, A3

Hidden around the back of the striking late-1920s functional-ist facade of the **Mánes Gallery** (Výstavní síň Mánes; www.galerie manes.com; admission free; ⏰10am-8pm Tue-Sun; 🚊5, 17), this gorgeous restaurant manages to be both welcoming and sophisticated, with its angular art-deco lines decorated with original ceiling frescoes by avant-garde Czech artist Emil Filla. The menu has

strong French influences, but also lends a gourmet touch to a handful of Czech classics. (📞730 150 772; www.manesrestaurant.cz; Masarykovo nábřeží 1; mains 245-395Kč; ⏰11am-midnight; 📶; 🚊5, 17)

Drinking

Cafe Louvre CAFE

10 ☕ MAP P112, C1

The French-style Cafe Louvre is arguably the most amenable of Prague's grand cafes, as popular today as it was in the early 1900s when it was frequented by the likes of Franz Kafka and Albert Einstein. The atmosphere is wonderfully olde worlde, and it serves good Czech food as well as coffee. Check out the billiard hall and the ground-floor art gallery. (📞724 054 055; www.cafelouvre.cz; 1st fl, Národní třída 22; ⏰8am-11.30pm Mon-Fri, from 9am Sat & Sun; 📶; Ⓜ Národní třída)

Kavárna Slavia CAFE

11 ☕ MAP P112, A1

The Slavia is the most famous of Prague's old cafes, a cherrywood-and-onyx shrine to art-deco elegance, with polished limestone-topped tables and big windows overlooking the river. It has been a celebrated literary meeting place since the early 20th century – Rainer Maria Rilke and Franz Kafka hung out here, and it was frequented by Václav Havel and other dissidents in the 1970s and '80s.

Prague's Grand Cafes

Prague is known for pubs, Vienna for its coffeehouses. Yet the Czech capital also boasts grand cafes that rival their Austrian cousins in looks (even if the actual coffee can't compete). The atmosphere, at least, is equivalent, and since the days of the Austro-Hungarian Empire, Prague's ornate, high-ceilinged coffeehouses have acted as public meeting spaces, hotbeds of political subversion and literary salons.

At various times Franz Kafka, playwright Karel Čapek (coiner of the term 'robot') and Albert Einstein all drank at **Cafe Louvre**, while across the road at **Kavárna Slavia**, patrons included Milan Kundera, Václav Havel and other writers, playwrights and filmmakers.

Today you might encounter performers from the National Theatre across the road, and mass tourism seems to have passed the place by. Best for a Turkish coffee and a slice of something nice on a rainy afternoon in the company of a good book. (📞224 218 493; www.cafeslavia.cz; Národní třída 1; ⏰8am-midnight Mon-Fri, 9am-midnight Sat & Sun; 📶; 🚊2, 9, 18, 22, 23)

U Fleků
BEER HALL

12 🚇 MAP P112, B3

A festive warren of drinking and dining rooms, U Fleků is a Prague institution, though it's usually clogged with tour groups high on oompah music and the tavern's home-brewed, slightly overpriced, 13° black beer (69Kč for 400mL). Purists grumble but go along anyway because the beer and atmosphere is good, though tourist prices have nudged out many locals. (📞224 934 019; www.ufleku.cz; Křemencová 11; ⏰10am-11pm; 📶; 🚊5)

Pivovarský Dům
BREWERY

13 🚇 MAP P112, D4

While the tourists flock to U Fleků, locals gather here to sample the Štěpán classic Czech lager that is produced on the premises, as well as wheat beer and a range of flavoured beers (including coffee, banana and nettle). The wood-panelled pub itself is a pleasant place to linger, decked out with polished copper vats and brewing implements. The pub also produces some interesting beer specialities such as beer soup and lager marmalade. The cheap lunch menu is also a reason to head here. (📞296 216 666; www.pivovarskydum.com; cnr Ječná & Lipová; ⏰11am-11.30pm; 🚊4, 6, 10, 13, 16, 22, 23)

Kavárna Velryba
CAFE

14 🚇 MAP P112, C2

The 'Whale' is a long-established arty cafe-bar – usually quiet enough to have a real conversation – with vegetarian-friendly snacks, a smoky back room and a basement art gallery. A clientele of Czech students, office workers and foreign backpackers attracted by low prices keep the place lively. (📞224 931 444; www.kavarnavelryba.cz; Opatovická 24; ⏰11am-11pm Mon-Fri, noon-11pm Sat & Sun; 🛜; 🚋3, 5, 6, 9, 14, 24)

Entertainment

National Theatre
THEATRE

15 ⭐ MAP P112, A1

The much-loved National Theatre provides a stage for traditional opera, drama and ballet by the likes of Smetana, Shakespeare and Tchaikovsky (the *Nutcracker* is hopelessly sold out before Christmas), sharing the programme alongside works by modern composers and playwrights. The box offices are in the Nový síň building next door, in the Kolowrat Palace (opposite the Estates Theatre) and at the State Opera.

A performance here is a quintessentially Czech experience. Smart casual attire, at a minimum, is required. (Národní divadlo; 📞224 901 448; www.narodni-divadlo.cz; Národní třída 2; ⏰box office 9am-6pm, from 10am Sat & Sun; 🚋2, 9, 18, 22, 23)

Reduta Jazz Club
JAZZ

16 ⭐ MAP P112, C1

The Reduta is Prague's oldest jazz club, actually founded in 1958 during the communist era. It was here in 1994 that former US president Bill Clinton famously jammed on a new saxophone presented to him by Václav Havel. It has an intimate setting, with smartly dressed patrons squeezing into tiered seats and lounges to soak up the big-band, swing and Dixieland atmosphere. (📞224 933 487; www.redutajazzclub.cz; Národní třída 20; ⏰7pm-1am; 🛜; Ⓜ Národní Třída)

Laterna Magika
PERFORMING ARTS

17 ⭐ MAP P112, A1

Laterna Magika has been wowing audiences since its first cutting-edge multimedia show caused a stir at the 1958 Brussels World Fair. Its imaginative blend of dance, music and projected images continues to pull in the crowds. Nová Scena, the futuristic building next to the National Theatre, has been home to Laterna Magika since it moved here from its birthplace in the Adria Palace in the mid-1970s. (📞224 901 417; www.narodni-divadlo.cz; Nová Scéna, Národní třída 4; tickets 260-690Kč; ⏰box office 9am-6pm Mon-Fri, 10am-6pm Sat & Sun; Ⓜ Národní Třída, 🚋2, 9, 18, 22, 23)

Image Theatre
PERFORMING ARTS

18 ⭐ MAP P112, C1

Established in 1989, this theatre company uses creative black-light theatre combined with pantomime, modern dance and video – not to mention liberal doses of slapstick – to tell its tales. The staging can be very effective, but the atmosphere is often dictated by audience reaction. (Divadlo Image; ☎222 314 448; www.image theatre.cz; Národní třída 25; ⏰box office 10am-8pm; Ⓜ Národní třída)

Wonderful Dvořák
CLASSICAL MUSIC

19 ⭐ MAP P112, E4

The pretty little Vila Amerika was built in 1717 as an aristocrat's immodest summer retreat. These days it's home to the **Dvořák Museum** (Muzeum Antonína Dvořáka; ☎774 845 823; www.nm.cz; adult/child 50/30Kč; ⏰10am-5pm Tue-Sun) and from May to October it stages performances of Dvořák's works by a chamber orchestra, complete with period costume. Book through the website. (Kouzelný Dvořák; www.musictheatre.cz; Ke Karlovu 20, Vila Amerika; tickets 595Kč; ⏰concerts 8pm Tue & Fri May-Oct; Ⓜ IP Pavlova)

Shopping

Náplavka Farmers Market
MARKET

20 🔒 MAP P112, A4

Stretching along the embankment from Trojická to Výtoň, this weekly market makes the most of its riverside setting with live music and outdoor tables scattered among stalls selling freshly baked bread, organic locally grown vegetables, homemade cakes and pastries, wild mushrooms (in season), herbs, flowers, wild honey, hot food, Czech cider, coffee and a range of arts and crafts.

The Náplavka is also used for other events and is the location of several summer barge bars as well as arches fronted by the largest opening circular glass windows in the world. When there's nothing going on, the embankment returns to the swans and gulls that call the Vltava home, and the odd jogger. (www.farmarsketrziste.cz; Rašínovo nábřeží; ⏰8am-2pm Sat; 🚊2, 3, 4, 10, 16, 21)

Walking Tour 🚶

Vyšehrad, Prague's Other Castle

The complex of buildings that make up Vyšehrad Citadel has played an important role in Czech history for more than 1000 years. While few of the ancient buildings have survived, the citadel is still viewed as Prague's spiritual home. For more information and an events calendar, see www. praha-vysehrad.cz.

Start Tábor Gate;
Ⓜ Vyšehrad

End Cafe Citadela;
🚊 Výtoň

Length 1.5km; one hour

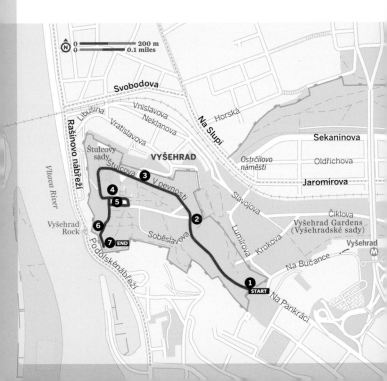

❶ Through the Old Gates

About 10 minutes on foot from the Vyšehrad metro station, heading west, you'll pass **Tábor Gate** and the remains of the original Gothic **Špička Gate**.

❷ Prague's Oldest Building

The 11th-century Romanesque **Rotunda of St Martin** is considered Prague's oldest surviving building. The door and frescoes date from a renovation in about 1880. It's only open during Mass.

❸ Into the Fortress

Through the **Brick Gate & Casements** (www.praha-vysehrad.cz; adult/child 60/30Kč; ⊘9.30am-6pm Apr-Oct, to 5pm Nov-Mar) are hidden vaults used for imprisonment and storing weapons when Vyšehrad served as a fortress in the 18th century. The underground **Gorlice Hall** holds some of Charles Bridge's original statues.

❹ Dvořák's Final Resting Place

The 600 graves (many with intricately designed headstones) in the lovely gardens of **Vyšehrad Cemetery** (admission free; ⊘8am-7pm May-Sep, reduced hours Oct-Apr) read like a who's who of Czech arts and letters, including musicians Antonín Dvořák and Bedřich Smetana and artist Alfons Mucha.

❺ Last Church Standing

The neo-Gothic **Church of Sts Peter & Paul** (adult/child 30/10Kč; ⊘9am-noon & 1-5pm Wed-Mon) was one of Vyšehrad's few structures to avoid destruction in 1420 during the Hussite religious wars. The current facade dates from the 19th century.

❻ Underground History

The atmospheric **Gothic Cellar** (Gotický sklep; adult/child 50/30Kč; ⊘9.30am-6pm Apr-Oct, to 5pm Nov-Mar) houses a worthwhile exhibit; its overview of the history of Prague's fortification helps put Vyšehrad's sights into perspective.

❼ Beer with a View

Along the fortress' southern ramparts, **Cafe Citadela** (www.facebook.com/cafecitadelavysehrad; ⊘9.30am-6pm Apr-Sep, 10am-5pm Wed-Sun Oct-Mar) is an outdoor beer garden with a relaxed vibe and nice views.

Explore ◈
Vinohrady &
Žižkov

Vinohrady and Žižkov are the yin and yang of residential Prague. Gentrified Vinohrady boasts high-ceilinged, art-nouveau apartment buildings and is popular with young professionals and expats. The 'people's republic' of Žižkov is historically working class, rebellious and revolutionary, famed for its numerous pubs.

The Short List

○ **Vinohrady and Žižkov nightlife (p132)** This duo of neighbourhoods provides some of the best nightlife in the Czech capital.

○ **Church of the Most Sacred Heart of Our Lord (p129)** This 1930s work by a Slovene architect is possibly Prague's weirdest church.

○ **National Monument (p128)** Visit Hussite warlord Jan Žižka on his mighty steed before getting the lowdown on some Czechoslovak history.

○ **TV Tower (p129)** Prague's tallest structure has a restaurant at the top and babies crawling up and down its concrete length.

○ **Riegrovy Sady (p129)** Known for its beer garden, this large park is a superb place to take it easy away from the tourist throngs.

Getting There & Around

🚋 Line 4, 10, 13, 16 or 22 to Náměstí Míru, line 11 or 13 to Jiřího z Poděbrad.

Ⓜ Line A to Náměstí Míru, Jiřího z Poděbrad or Flora.

Neighbourhood Map on p126

TV Tower (p129) with *Babies* by David Černý KATATONIA82/SHUTTERSTOCK ©

Drinking Tour 🍷

Bar Tour of Vinohrady & Žižkov

In Prague, there's no better place to make a night of it: Žižkov, on one side, proudly claims to have more pubs per square metre than anywhere else in the world; on the other side, classy Vinohrady is home to some serious wine and cocktail bars, where the staff really know how to mix a drink.

Start Vinohradský Parlament; Ⓜ Náměstí Míru

End Bukowski's; 🚋 Lipanská

Length 2.5km; one hour

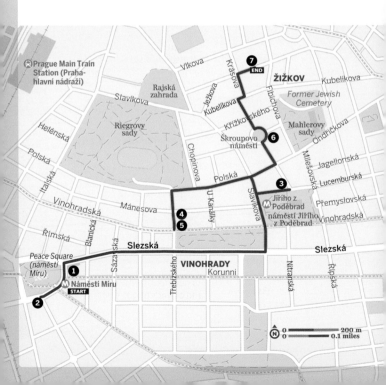

❶ Put Something In Your Stomach

A sturdy meal is always a good idea if a night of drinking is on the cards. **Vinohradský Parlament** (p130), on Peace Square (náměstí Míru), offers excellent modern twists on Czech pub food, paired with the best beers offered by the Staropramen brewery.

❷ Night at the 'Museum'

Just across Peace Square, the **Prague Beer Museum** (www. praguebeermuseum.com; Americká 43; ⏰11am-2am Mon-Thu, noon-3am Fri & Sat; 🛜) – actually a pub – offers 30 regional Czech beers on tap, so once you've had your fill of Staropramen, see what else the country has to offer.

❸ French Wine with Style

One metro stop away, at Jiřího z Poděbrad, **Le Caveau** (www. broz-d.cz; náměstí Jiřího z Poděbrad 9 ⏰8am-10.30pm Mon-Fri, from 9am Sat, 2-8.30pm Sun) offers the city's best selection of French wines and upmarket cheeses and snacks to match. Wine drinkers may want to start the night right here.

❹ Classy Cocktails at Bar & Books

At this stage, you can stay classy or go crazy. For classy, **Bar & Books Mánesova** (www.barand books.cz; Mánesova 64; ⏰6pm-3am Mon-Sat, to 2am Sun) is a sensuous cocktail lounge featuring lush, library-themed decor, top-shelf liquor and live music some nights.

❺ Crazy Dancing at Termix

If crazy is the order of the night and it's after 10pm, gay-friendly **Termix** (p133) is the place to head. It stays open until 5am or so on weekends, so no need to move on if this is your scene.

❻ Beer at U Sadu

For more working-class libations, the congenial neighbourhood pub **U Sadu** (www.usadu.cz; Škroupovo náměstí 5; ⏰8am-4am Tue-Sat, to 2am Sun & Mon) is supremely popular with old locals, dread-locked students and expats alike. Staff also run the kitchen past midnight, so if you're craving a snack, this may be your only option.

❼ Nightcap at Bukowski's

On the Žižkov street that's reckoned to have more drinking dens per metre than anywhere else in Prague, **Bukowski's** (www.facebook. com/bukowskisbar; Bořivojova 86; ⏰7pm-3am), named after the hard-drinking American poet Charles Bukowski, is a cut above its neighbours. Expect cool tunes and confident cocktails.

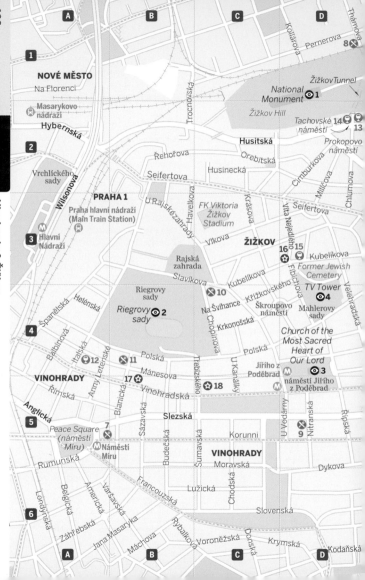

A

B

C

D

1

NOVÉ MĚSTO
Na Florenci

Masarykovo nádraží
Hybernská

ŽižkovTunnel

National Monument ⊙1

Žižkov Hill

Tachovské 14 ⊙
náměstí 13

Pernerova 8

Kollárova

Trhanova

2

Vrchlického sady

Wilsonova

Řehořova

Seifertova

Husitská

Orebitská

Husinecká

Prokopovo náměstí

Trocnovská

Cimburkova

Milíčova

Chlumova

PRAHA 1

Praha hlavní nádraží
(Main Train Station)

U Rajské zahrady

Havelkova

FK Viktoria Žižkov Stadium

Vlkova

Krásová

Seifertova

3

Hlavní Nádraží

ŽIŽKOV

16 ⊙ 15

Kubelíkova

Former Jewish Cemetery

Rajská zahrada

Slavíkova

Kubelíkova

Křižíkovského

TV Tower ⊙4

Vita Nejedlého

Fibichova

Velehradská

Riegrovy sady

Riegrovy sady ⊙2

Na Švihance

Škroupovo náměstí

Mahlerovy sady

4

Španělská

Helénská

Balbínova

Italská

Anny Letenské

⊙12 ⊙11

Polská

Mánesova

17 ⊙

⊙18

Vinohradská

Chopinova

Krkonošská

Polská

Třebízského

U Kanálky

Church of the Most Sacred Heart of Our Lord

Jiřího z Poděbrad

náměstí Jiřího z Poděbrad ⊙3

VINOHRADY

Římská

Slezská

Sázavská

Budečská

Šumavská

Korunní

U Vodárny

Nitranská

Řipská

5

Anglická

Peace Square (náměstí Míru)

7

Náměstí Míru

Rumunská

VINOHRADY

Moravská

9

Dykova

6

Londýnská

Belgická

Americká

Varšavská

Záhřebská

Jana Masaryka

Máchova

Francouzská

Rybalkova

Lužická

Chodská

Voroněžská

Slovenská

Donská

Krymská

Kodaňská

A

B

C

D

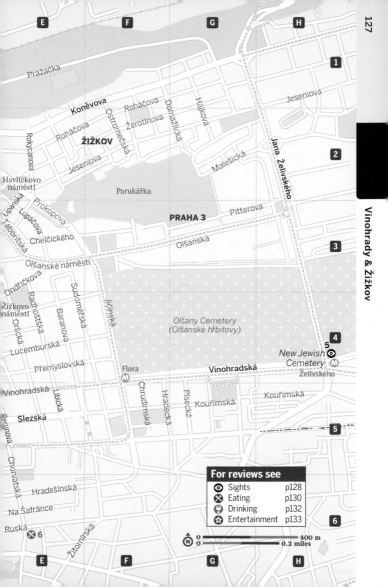

Vinohrady & Žižkov

ŽIŽKOV

PRAHA 3

Parukářka

Olšany Cemetery
(Olšanské hřbitovy)

New Jewish
Cemetery

For reviews see

👁	Sights	p128
✖	Eating	p130
🍺	Drinking	p132
★	Entertainment	p133

0   400 m
0   0.2 miles

Sights

National Monument   MUSEUM

1 👁 MAP P126, D1

While this monument's massive functionalist structure has all the elegance of a nuclear power station, the interior is a spectacular extravaganza of polished art-deco marble, gilt and mosaics, and is home to a fascinating museum of 20th-century Czechoslovak history.

Although, strictly speaking, not a legacy of the communist era – it was completed in the 1930s – the huge monument atop Žižkov Hill is, in the minds of most Praguers over a certain age, inextricably linked with the Communist Party of Czechoslovakia, and in particular with Klement Gottwald, the country's first 'worker-president'. The monument's central hall – home to a dozen marble sarcophagi that once bore the remains of communist luminaries – houses a moving **war memorial** with sculptures by Jan Sturša. There are exhibits recording the founding of the Czechoslovak Republic in 1918, WWII, the 1948 coup, the Soviet invasion of 1968 (poignant newsreel footage and a handful of personal possessions record the tragic story of Jan Palach, who set himself on fire to protest the Soviet invasion) and the Velvet Revolution of 1989. Upstairs you can visit the Ceremonial Hall and the Presidential Lounge. But the most grimly fascinating part of the museum is the Frankenstein-like **laboratory** beneath the Liberation Hall, where scientists once battled to prevent Gottwald's corpse from decomposing. On display in a glass-walled sarcophagus by day, his body was lowered into this white-tiled crypt every night for another frantic round of maintenance and repair. In the corner is the refrigerated chamber where Gottwald spent his nights (now occupied by the shattered remains

How the Tower Got Its Babies

It was Czech artist-provocateur David Černý who first placed the creepy babies on the side of the Žižkov TV Tower (pictured, p122) in an installation called *Miminka* (Mummy), timed for Prague's reign as European Capital of Culture in 2000. The babies came down at the end of that year, but the resultant public outcry saw them reinstated, and it seems they're now a permanent fixture.

We're no art critics here, but the babies *are* sporting slotted faces, like a USB drive, lending at least one interpretation that the installation is intended as a commentary on our overdependence on media for sustenance. Or maybe not. Come to think of it, the tower *does* look a bit like a baby's bottle…

of his sarcophagus), and in the adjoining room is a phalanx of 1950s control panels, switches and instruments that once monitored the great leader's temperature and humidity.Interesting temporary exhibitions are also held here, mostly on a Czechoslovak history theme. (Národní Památník na Vítkově; ☎224 497 600; www.nm.cz; U Památníku 1900, Žižkov; exhibition only adult/child 80/60Kč, roof terrace 80/50Kč, combined ticket 120/80Kč; ⏱10am-6pm Thu-Sun; 🚌133, 175, 207)

Riegrovy sady GARDENS

2 ◉ MAP P126, B4

Vinohrady's largest and prettiest park was designed as a classic English garden in the 19th century, and it's still a good place to put down a blanket and chill out. The bluff towards the back of the park affords photo-ops of Prague Castle. (Rieger Gardens; entrance on Chopinova, across from Na Švíhance, Vinohrady; admission free; ⏱24hr; Ⓜ Jiřího z Poděbrad, 🚌11, 13)

Church of the Most Sacred Heart of Our Lord CHURCH

3 ◉ MAP P126, D4

This church from 1932 is one of Prague's most original pieces of 20th-century architecture. It's the work of Jože Plečnik, a Slovene architect who also worked on Prague Castle. The church is inspired by Egyptian temples and early Christian basilicas. It's usually only open to the public during Mass. (Kostel Nejsvětějšího Srdce Páně; ☎222 727 713; www.srdcepane.cz; náměstí Jiřího z Poděbrad 19, Vinohrady; admission free; ⏱services 8am & 6pm Mon-Sat, 9am, 11am & 6pm Sun; Ⓜ Jiřího z Poděbrad, 🚌11, 13)

TV Tower TOWER

4 ◉ MAP P126, D4

Prague's tallest landmark – and depending on your tastes, either its ugliest or its most futuristic feature – is the 216m-tall TV Tower, erected between 1985 and 1992. More bizarre than its architecture are the 10 giant crawling babies that appear to be exploring the outside of the tower – an installation called **Miminka** (Mummy; www.davidcerny.cz), by artist David Černý. (Televizní Vysílač; ☎210 320 081; www.towerpark.cz; Mahlerovy sady 1, Žižkov; adult/child/family 250/160/590Kč; ⏱observation decks 8am-midnight; Ⓜ Jiřího z Poděbrad)

New Jewish Cemetery CEMETERY

5 ◉ MAP P126, H4

Franz Kafka is buried in this cemetery, which opened around 1890 when the older Jewish cemetery – at the foot of the TV Tower – was closed. To find **Kafka's grave**, follow the main avenue east (signposted), turn right at row 21, then left at the wall; it's at the end of the 'block'. Fans make a pilgrimage on 3 June, the anniversary of his death. The entrance is beside Želivského metro station; men should cover their heads (yarmulkes are available at the gate).

Not Big in Belgium

Design buffs beware. When Czechs talk about 'Brussels style', they're not referring to Belgian art nouveau or anything related to Henry Van de Velde. Rather, they're harking back to a heyday of their own national design when, despite the constraints of working under a communist regime, Czechoslovakia triumphed with its circular restaurant pavilion at the 1958 Brussels Expo. More than 100 local designers took away awards, including porcelain designer Jaroslav Ježek, who won the Grand Prix for his Elka coffee service. The aesthetics of the time were similar to what you see at **Café Kaaba** (p132). For a more authentic take, visit **Veletržní Palác** (p136).

Last admission is 30 minutes before closing. (Nový židovské hřbitov; ☎ 226 235 216; www.kehil aprag.cz; Izraelská 1, Žižkov; admission free; ⏱ 9am-5pm Sun-Thu, to 2pm Fri Apr-Oct, 9am-4pm Sun-Thu, to 2pm Fri Nov-Mar, closed on Jewish holidays; Ⓜ Želivského)

Eating

Benjamin INTERNATIONAL €€€

6 MAP P126, E6

Vršovice may be low on cool restaurants, but it does have one of Prague's most prized fine-dining establishments. Benjamin serves just 10 guests a night at its horseshoe-shaped counter. The choice is a five- or eight-course menu (wine pairing 530/990Kč), featuring fancy dishes inspired by old Czech recipes. (☎ 774 141 432; www.benjamin14.cz; Norská 602/14, Vršovice; 5-/8-course menu 1290/1890Kč; ⏱ 5.30-7.30pm & 8.15-11.30pm Wed-Sat; 🚊 4, 13, 22)

Vinohradský Parlament CZECH €

7 MAP P126, A5

This clean, bright pub features both a handsome early-modern, art-nouveau interior and a daring, inventive cooking staff who are willing to look beyond the standard pork and duck to other traditional Czech staples such as goose, rabbit, and boar. Perfect for both lunch and dinner, but phone ahead to book a table as it's often jammed. (☎ 224 250 403; www.vinohradskyparlament.cz; Korunní 1, Vinohrady; mains 180-250Kč; ⏱ 10.45am-11pm Mon, to 11.30pm Tue & Wed, to midnight Thu & Fri, 11.30am-midnight Sat, to 11pm Sun; 🛜 Ⓜ Náměstí Míru, 🚊 4, 11, 13, 16, 10, 22)

Hostinec U Tunelu CZECH €

8 MAP P126, D1

At the mouth of the pedestrian tunnel linking Žižkov with Karlín, this weekday-only, retro-styled

1920s tavern serves lunch specials containing exotic ingredients such as tzatziki, Gorgonzola and avocado until 2pm, after which it reverts to Czech beer snacks such as fried cheese, pickled sausages and beef with horseradish. The simple woody dining room is perfect for sipping a Konrad or Kocour beer. Cash only. (224 815 801; www.utunelu.cz; Thámova 1; mains & snacks 75-149Kč; 11am-11pm Mon-Fri; Křižíkova, 3, 8, 24)

Kofein

SPANISH €€

9 MAP P126, D5

One of the hottest restaurants in town is this tapas place not far from the Jiřího z Poděbrad metro station. Descend into a lively space to see a red-faced chef minding the busy grill. Local faves include

marinated trout with horseradish and pork belly confit with celeriac. Service is prompt and friendly. Book ahead. (273 132 145; www.ikofein.cz; Nitranská 9, Vinohrady; plates 95-135Kč; 11am-midnight Mon-Fri, from 5pm Sat & Sun; Jiřího z Poděbrad, 10, 11, 13, 16)

The Tavern

BURGERS €

10 MAP P126, C4

This cosy sit-down burger joint is the dream of a husband-and-wife team of American expats who wanted to create the perfect burger using organic products and free-range, grass-fed beef. Great pulled-pork sandwiches and different kinds of veggie burgers, too. You can request a reservation on the website. (www.thetavern.cz; Chopinova 26, Vinohrady; burgers

Café Kaaba (p132)

150-350Kč; ⏱11.30am-10pm Mon-Fri, from 11am Sat & Sun; 🛜; Ⓜ Jiřího z Poděbrad, 🚋 11, 13)

Pastička CZECH €€

11 🍴 MAP P126, B4

A warm, inviting ground-floor pub with a little garden out the back, Pastička is great for a beer or a meal. The interior design is part 1920s Prague and part Irish pub. Most come for the beer, but the mix of international and traditional Czech dishes is very good. (📞 222 253 228; www.pastickapraha.cz; Blanická 25, Vinohrady; mains 150-400Kč; ⏱11am-11.30pm Mon-Sat; 🛜; Ⓜ Jiřího z Poděbrad, 🚋 11, 13)

Drinking

Café Kaaba CAFE

12 🍺 MAP P126, A4

Café Kaaba is a stylish little cafe-bar with retro furniture and pastel-coloured decor that comes straight out of the 1959 Ideal Homes Exhibition. It serves up excellent coffee made with freshly ground imported beans. (📞 reservations 222 254 021; www.kaaba.cz; Mánesova 20, Vinohrady; ⏱8am-2am Mon-Fri, from 9am Sat, 10am-midnight Sun; 🛜; 🚋 11, 13)

U Slovanské Lípy PUB

13 🍺 MAP P126, D2

A classic Žižkov pub, plain and unassuming in and out, 'At the Linden Trees' (the linden is a Czech national emblem) is something of a place of pilgrimage for beer lovers.

The reason is its range of artisan brews from all over the country. This can include anything from Krušnohor from the remote north-west, to Benedikt from Prague's Břevnov Monastery. (📞 734 743 094; www.uslovanskelipy.cz; Tachovské náměstí 6, Žižkov; ⏱11am-midnight; 🛜; 🚋 133, 175, 207)

Planeta Žižkov PUB

14 🍺 MAP P126, D2

The legendary Planet is a wonderful Žižkov boozer serving dewy tankards of Urquell and Gambrinus as well as elephantine portions of Czech pub-resto food such as fried cheese, pork knuckle and goulash with dumplings. The eclectic interior runs from Viktoria Žižkov football scarves to jumble-sale furniture, and the clientele is mostly Žižkováci (natives of the planet). (📞 222 780 173; www.planetazizkov.cz; Tachovské náměstí 1; ⏱11am-1am Mon-Sat, to midnight Sun; 🚋 133, 175, 207)

U Kurelů PUB

15 🍺 MAP P126, D3

Originally opened in 1907, this well-kept, more civilised Žižkov tavern has changed only slightly since 1989, still sporting its typical wood inventory and dim lighting. Though the menu of burgers, nachos and quesadillas would have seemed like something from outer space in those days, the Urquell and Gambrinus have remained. There's also a long cocktail and non-alcoholic list. (www.ukurelu.cz; Chvalova 1, Žižkov; ⏱5-11pm; 🛜; 🚋 1, 5, 9, 13, 15, 26)

Absinth(e) Makes the Heart Grow Fonder

For many visitors, Prague is synonymous with absinth. That's been the case since the 1990s, when Czech drinks firm Hills cleverly revived this long-banned, legendary and allegedly hallucinatory 19th-century French-Swiss tipple. Today, however, the Swiss and French have resumed production of the genuine 'green fairy', and true connoisseurs hold their noses when it comes to replica 'Czechsinths'.

What's the difference? Most Czech brands use oil to mix the active ingredient, wormwood, into the liquid, instead of properly distilling it. If you'll be packing a bottle in your suitcase, try the pricey but excellent Czech-made Toulouse Lautrec (about 1200Kč at shops around town).

Entertainment

Palác Akropolis
LIVE MUSIC

16 ⭐ MAP P126, D3

The Akropolis is a Prague institution, a labyrinthine, sticky-floored shrine to alternative music and drama. Its various performance spaces host a smorgasbord of musical and cultural events, from DJs and string quartets to Macedonian Roma bands, local rock gods and visiting talent – Marianne Faithfull, the Flaming Lips and the Strokes have all played here. (☎296 330 913; www.palacakropolis.cz; Kubelíkova 27, Žižkov; ticket prices vary; ⏰7pm-5am; 🛜; 🚊5, 9, 15, 26)

Techtle Mechtle
CLUB

17 ⭐ MAP P126, B5

A popular cellar dance bar on Vinohrady's main drag. The name translates to 'hanky panky' in Czech, and that's what most of the swank people who come here are after. In addition to a well-tended cocktail bar, you'll find a decent restaurant and dance floor, and occasional special events. Arrive early to get a good table. (☎222 250 143; www.techtle-mechtle.cz; Vinohradská 47, Vinohrady; ⏰6pm-4am Tue-Thu, to 5am Fri & Sat; 🛜; 🅜Náměstí Míru, 🚊4, 10, 13, 16, 22)

Termix
CLUB

18 ⭐ MAP P126, C5

Termix is one of Prague's most popular gay dance clubs, with an industrial hi-tech vibe (lots of shiny steel, glass and plush sofas) and a young crowd that includes as many tourists as locals. The smallish dance floor fills up fast and you may have to queue to get in. (☎222 710 462; www.club-termix.cz; Třebízského 4a, Vinohrady; ⏰10pm-6am Wed-Sat; 🅜Jiřího z Poděbrad, 🚊11, 13)

Explore ◈
Holešovice

In Holešovice, you start to appreciate Prague as a genuine working city. Though sections of this former industrial quarter remain somewhat run-down, the neighbourhood has been slowly gentrifying. The hilltop beer garden at Letná is a relaxing spot on a warm summer evening, while the National Gallery's impressive holdings at Veletržní Palác may make for Prague's most underrated museum.

The Short List

○ **Veletržní Palác (p136)** *Top billing in this neighbourhood goes to the National Gallery's modern- and contemporary-art exhibition.*

○ **Prague Zoo (p139)** *The best zoo in the country can be found on a steep hill on the north bank of the River Vltava.*

○ **National Technical Museum (p139)** *One of the best places in the capital to take the children, especially on a rainy day.*

○ **Letná Gardens (p139)** *Overlooking the old centre, this park is a great place to grab a beer or unfurl a picnic blanket.*

○ **Cool eating and nightlife (p140)** *Holešovice is the latest Prague suburb to be awarded the title 'up-and-coming'.*

Getting There & Around

🚊 Lines 1, 8, 12, 25, 26 to Letenské náměstí; lines 1, 6, 8, 12, 25, 26 to Strossmayerovo náměstí.

Ⓜ Line C to Vltavská or Nádraží Holešovice.

Neighbourhood Map on p138

Schwarzenberg Palace (p137) FLIK47/SHUTTERSTOCK ©

Top Experience 📷

Get Your Art Fix at Veletržní Palác

The National Gallery's collection of art from the 19th, 20th and 21st centuries is a must for art lovers, particularly fans of impressionism, constructivism, Dadaism and surrealism. The holdings are strong on French impressionists, early modern masters such as Schiele, Klimt and Picasso, and the generation of Czech artists working in the 1920s and '30s.

◉ MAP P138, C3

www.ngprague.cz

Dukelských hrdinů 47

adult/concession 220/120Kč

🕙 10am-6pm Tue & Thu-Sun, to 8pm Wed

Ⓜ Vltavská, 🚃 1, 6, 8, 12, 14, 17, 25, 26

French Collection

Thanks to a strong Bohemian interest in French painting, the palace's 3rd floor has an impressive collection of 19th- and 20th-century French art. Artists represented include Monet, Gauguin, Cézanne, Picasso, Delacroix and Rodin. Look for Gauguin's *Flight* and Van Gogh's *Green Wheat*.

Avant-Garde Czech Art

The museum's display of 20th-century Czech art (also on the 3rd floor) is one of the country's finest. Standouts include the geometric works by František Kupka, and cubist paintings, ceramics and design by several different artists – these paintings show an interesting parallel with the concurrent art scene in Paris. On the 2nd floor, look for the most contemporary Czech works across several genres.

Female Imagery in the International Collection

The 20th-century international collection, on the 1st floor, boasts works by some major names: Klimt, Schiele, Sherman and Miró, to name a few. Two highlights take on feminine themes: Klimt's luscious, vibrantly hued *The Virgins* and Schiele's much darker, foreboding *Pregnant Woman and Death*.

Prague's National Gallery

The Veletržní Palác is just one branch of the National Gallery. Buy a 500Kč ticket for entry to all of the gallery's buildings hosting permanent exhibitions, including the Schwarzenberg Palace, Kinský Palace and the Convent of St Agnes.

★ **Top Tips**

o The museum is huge. If you only have an hour or two, just hit the highlights listed here.

o Children and young adults up to 26 years of age enjoy free admission.

o Pick up Prague postcards or souvenirs at the museum shop.

✗ **Take a Break**

The museum cafe, located on the ground floor and open during museum hours, is convenient for a coffee.

Just across the road is **U Houbaře** (☎720 625 923; www.u-houbare.cz; Dukelských Hrdinů 30; ⊙11am-midnight; ⓂVltavská, ⓇR1, 6, 8, 12, 14, 17, 25, 26), an old-school pub with a cheap menu.

Holešovice Get Your Art Fix at Veletržní Palác

Holešovice

For reviews see
- Top Experiences p136
- ◉ Sights p139
- ✕ Eating p140
- ◑ Drinking p141
- ✷ Entertainment p143

500 m
0.25 miles

Vrbenského

Ortenovo náměstí

Poupětova

DOX Centre for Contemporary Art

Plynární

U Měst' pivovaru

Přístavní

Osadní

U průhonu

Dělnická

HOLEŠOVICE

Komunardů

Tovární

Tusarova

Jateční

Bubenské nábřeží

Vltava River

Argentinská

Za viaduktem

Argentinská

Janovského

Žst Praha Bubny

Vltavská

Ostrov Štvanice

Jankovcova

Nádraží Holešovice

Praha-Holešovice zastávka

Partyzánská

Železničářů

PRAHA 7

Bubenská

Veletržní

Za elektrárnou

U Výstaviště

Strojnická

Vystaviště Exhibition Grounds

Výstaviště tram stop

Dukelských hrdinů

Veletržní Palác

Heřmanova

Veverkova

Podplukovníka Sochora

Strossmayerovo náměstí

Kostelní

Hlávkův Bridge (Hlávkův most)

nábřeží Kpt Jaroše

Stromovka

PRAHA 7

U akademie

U studánky

Umělecká

Kamenická

Heřmanova

Milady Horákové

Letohradská

Kostelní

Stromovka Park

Šmeralová

Veletržní

Letenské náměstí

Jiřečkova

Františka Křížka

Letenský Tunnel

Letná Gardens 2

Nad štolou

Čechova

National Technical Museum

Letná

Letná Gardens (Letenské sady)

Korunovační

LETNÁ

Sights

National Technical Museum
MUSEUM

1 MAP P138, B4

Prague's family-friendly National Technical Museum got a high-tech renovation in 2012 and is a dazzling presentation of the country's industrial heritage. The exhibits here are anything but dull. Start in the main hall, filled to the rafters with historic planes, trains and automobiles. There are separate halls devoted to displays on astronomy, photography, printing and architecture. (Národní Technické Muzeum; ☏ 220 399 111; www.ntm.cz; Kostelní 42; adult/concession 250/130Kč; ☺ 9am-6pm Tue-Sun; P ᵗ; ☐ 1, 6, 8, 12, 14, 17, 25, 26)

Letná Gardens
PARK

2 MAP P138, B4

Lovely Letná Gardens occupies a bluff over the Vltava River, north of the Old Town, and has postcard-perfect views out over the city, river and bridges. It's ideal for walking, jogging and drinking at a popular beer garden (p141) at the eastern end of the park. From the Old Town, find the entrance up a steep staircase at the northern end of Pařížská ulice (across the bridge). Alternatively, take the tram to Letenské náměstí and walk south for about 10 minutes. (Letenské sady; admission free; ☺ 24hr; ᵗ; ☐ 1, 8, 12, 25, 26 to Letenské náměstí)

Výstaviště Exhibition Grounds
CULTURAL CENTRE

3 MAP P138, C1

This sprawling, somewhat neglected area of attractions and buildings was first laid out for the 1891 Jubilee Exhibition. These days it holds mainly trade fairs (see the website for a calendar), but also has a branch of the National Museum and the city's biggest aquarium. (☏ 220 103 111; www.incheba.cz; Areál Výstaviště, Bubeneč; ☺ 9am-11pm; ☐ 12, 17)

Prague Zoo

Prague's attractive **zoo** (Zoo Praha; ☏ 296 112 230; www.zoopraha.cz; U Trojského zámku 120, Troja; adult/concession/family 200/150/600Kč; ☺ 9am-9pm Jun-Aug, to 6pm Apr, May, Sep & Oct, to 5pm Mar, to 4pm Nov-Feb; ᵗ; ☐ 112, M Nádraží Holešovice) is set on 60 hectares of wooded grounds on the banks of the Vltava. It makes for a great outing for kids. There are sizeable collections of giraffes and gorillas, but pride of place goes to a herd of rare horses. Attractions include a miniature cable car and a big play area.

Stromovka Park

Prague's largest central park, **Stromovka** (Královská obora; Map p138, A2; entry at Výstaviště or Nad Královskou oborou 21, Bubeneč; ⏰24hr; 🚊1, 8, 12, 25, 26), was once a medieval hunting ground for royals; now it's popular with strollers, joggers, cyclists and inline skaters. Kids can climb on the huge gnarled branches of ancient fallen trees, or play at one of several playgrounds – and adults will appreciate the lavish tulip display in spring.

Eating

The Eatery   CZECH €€

4 🍴 MAP P138, F1

The Eatery is the best restaurant in eastern Holešovice, hands-down. The sophisticated space, bathed in steel and tones of grey, shuttles out local, seasonal dishes from an open kitchen. Think Czech food, but with a modern twist – braised beef with potato purée and bone-marrow crumble, or pheasant. The wine menu is delightfully long. (📞603 945 236; www.theeatery. cz; U Uranie 18; mains 200-350Kč; ⏰11.30am-3.30pm & 5.30-11pm Tue-Fri, 5.30-11pm Sat; 📶; Ⓜ Nádraží Holešovice, 🚊6, 12)

Salt'n'Pepa Kitchen   BURGERS €

5 🍴 MAP P138, C3

Salt'n'Pepa's gourmet burgers are a big hit in Holešovice. Don't expect standard bun-and-patty action here – variations include halloumi, pulled pork and buttermilk fried chicken. Drinks are served in big cups with metal straws, fitting perfectly to the restaurant's diner-inspired set-up. (📞704 179 803; www.saltnpepa.cz; Milady Horákové 22; burgers 175-195Kč; ⏰11am-10pm Mon-Tue, to 11pm Wed-Fri, 10am-10pm Sat, to 10am-8pm Sun; 🚊1, 6, 8, 12, 17, 25, 26)

Pivovar Marina   ITALIAN €€€

6 🍴 MAP P138, F1

An unlikely but welcome combination: an excellent Czech microbrewery and proper Italian cooking. For beers, the wheat beer and 10° Přístavní lager are certainly worth trying. The food includes high-end pasta and mains such as Wagyu steak. During the warmer months, the outdoor tables afford relaxing views over the river. (📞220 571 183; www.pivovarmarina. cz; Jankovcova 12; mains 490-2500Kč; ⏰11am-midnight (kitchen to 11pm); 📶; 🚊6, 12)

Phill's Corner   INTERNATIONAL €

7 🍴 MAP P138, F2

This bright, modern corner restaurant draws design inspiration from Holešovice's industrial past and its culinary cues from kitchens around the world, including flavours from Asia and the Middle East. The daily lunch menu of soup and a main course for around 150Kč is a great deal. (☎731 836 988; www.phillscorner.cz; Komunardů 32; mains 135-180Kč; ⏰7.30am-10pm Mon-Fri, 9am-10pm Sun; 🛜📶; 🚊1, 6, 12, 14, 25)

Tràng An Restaurace
VIETNAMESE €

8 MAP P138, E3

Holešovice's **Prague Market** (☎220 800 592; Bubenské nábřeží 306; ⏰7.30am-5pm Mon-Fri, to 2pm Sat) is in a dreary state, but this low-key Vietnamese restaurant is a solid reason to turn up. Queue with everyone else at the counter and choose from a large picture menu on the wall. There's plenty of indoor seating and outside picnic tables in nice weather. Try to visit before or after typical meal times to avoid a wait. (☎220 560 041; www.prazska-trznice.cz/trang -an; Bubenské nábřeží 306, Bldg 5, Holešovická tržnice/Pražská tržnice; mains 100-130Kč; ⏰10am-8pm Mon-Sat; Ⓜ Vltavská, 🚊1, 12, 14, 25)

Drinking

Letná Beer Garden
BEER GARDEN

9 🚐 MAP P138, B4

No accounting of watering holes in Holešovice would be complete without a nod towards the city's best beer garden, with an amazing panorama, situated at the eastern end of the Letná Gardens (p139). Buy a takeaway beer

Cross Club (p143)

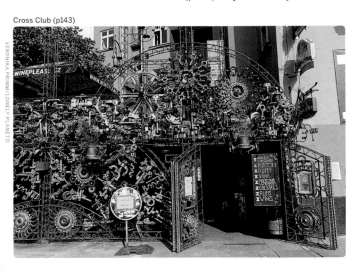

DOX Centre for Contemporary Art

Just a short tram ride from Veletržní Palác, the **DOX Centre for Contemporary Art** (Map p138, F1; ☎295 568 123; www.dox.cz; Poupětova 1; adult/concession 180/90Kč; ☺10am-6pm Mon, Sat & Sun, 11am-7pm Wed & Fri, 11am-9pm Thu; ⓂNádraží Holešovice, 🚊6, 12) is a private gallery and museum that's trying to re-establish Holešovice's reputation as the repository of Prague's best modern art. The minimalist multilevel building occupies an entire corner block, providing Prague's most capacious gallery space, studded with a diverse range of thought-provoking contemporary art and photography. Don't miss DOX's excellent cafe and bookshop.

from a small kiosk and grab a picnic table. Kiosks also sell small food items such as chips and sandwiches. (☎233 378 200; www.letenskyzamecek.cz; Letenské sady 341; ☺11am-11pm May-Sep; 🚊1, 8, 12, 25, 26)

Vnitroblock

CAFE

 10 🚇 MAP P138, F3

Hidden in the back of an industrial building, Vnitroblock is the coolest daytime hangout in Holešovice. There's a pop-up kitchen, sneaker store and cafe, but contemporary art on the exposed brick walls makes it an art gallery, too. Dogs lounge beneath tables while their owners work on laptops, but there's also plenty of space for kicking back. (☎770 101 231; www.vnitroblock.cz; Tusarova 31; ☺noon-10pm Mon, 9am-10pm Tue-Sat, 9am-8pm Sun; 🛜🍽; 🚊1, 6, 12, 14, 25)

Cobra

BAR

11 🚇 MAP P138, C3

This all-purpose cafe, lunch spot and late-night bar has something for everyone: very good coffee and tea, microbrews and well-made cocktails. There's also an open kitchen at the back that serves up a daily soup and main-course lunch. The menu is filled with vegan options. (☎777 355 876; www.barcobra.cz; Milady Horákové 8; ☺8am-1am Mon, to 2am Tue-Fri, 10am-2am Sat, 10am-1am Sun; 🛜; 🚊1, 6, 8, 12, 17, 25, 26)

Fraktal

BAR

12 🚇 MAP P138, A3

This subterranean space under a corner house near Letenské náměstí is easily the friendliest bar this side of the Vltava. This is especially true for English speakers, as Fraktal over the years has served as a kind of unofficial expat watering hole. There's also good bar fare such as burgers (mains 140Kč to 300Kč). The only drawback is the early closing time (last orders at 11.30pm). (☎ 777 794 094; www. facebook.com/fraktalbar; Šmeralová 1, Bubeneč; ⏱ 11am-midnight; 🛜; 🚋 1, 8, 12, 25, 26)

Kavárna Liberál CAFE

13 🗺 MAP P138, D3

This Viennese-style coffee house captures something of Prague in the 1920s. By day, it's a quiet spot for coffee and connecting with wi-fi; evenings bring out a more pub-like feel. There are occasional live bands in the basement. The menu includes coffee, beer and wine, and light foods such as salads and omelettes. Often it will have excellent sweets such as cheesecake and apple strudel. (☎ 732 355 445; www.facebook.com/ kavarnaliberal; Heřmanova 6; ⏱ 8am-midnight Mon-Fri, from 9am Sat, from 10am Sun; 🛜; Ⓜ Vltavská, 🚋 1, 6, 8, 12, 14, 17, 25, 26)

Entertainment

Cross Club CLUB

14 🗺 MAP P138, E1

An industrial club in every sense: the setting in an industrial zone; the thumping music (both DJs and live acts); and the structure – a must-see maze of gadgets, shafts, cranks and pipes, many of which move and pulsate with light to the music. The programme includes occasional live music, theatre performances and art happenings.

Also has a cafe, open 2pm to 2am. (☎ cafe reservations 775 541 430; www.crossclub.cz; Plynární 23; live shows 100-200Kč; ⏱ 6pm-5am; 🛜; Ⓜ Nádraží Holešovice, 🚋 6, 12)

Jatka 78 ARTS CENTER

15 🗺 MAP P138, E3

This alternative art space, housed in a former slaughterhouse in Holešovice's Prague Market (p141), stages performances from dance to circus and acrobatics. Many shows are kid-friendly. It's worth grabbing a bite at the bistro before or after – the meals, including sandwiches and pasta, and reasonably priced, and there's a family play area, too. (☎ reservations 775 402 027; www. jatka78.cz; Bubenské nábřeží 306, Hall 17, Pražská tržnice; ⏱ box office 10am-midnight Mon-Sat, 1½hr before performances Sun; 👶; Ⓜ Vltavská, 🚋 1, 12, 14, 25)

La Fabrika PERFORMING ARTS

16 🗺 MAP P138, F2

The name refers to a 'factory', but this is actually a former paint warehouse that's been converted into an experimental perfor-mance space. Depending on the night, there's live music (jazz or cabaret), theatre, dance or film. Consult the website for the latest programme. Try to reserve in advance as shows typically sell out. (☎ box office 774 417 644; www. lafabrika.cz; Komunardů 30; tickets 200-400Kč; ⏱ box office 2-7.30pm Mon-Fri; 🚋 1, 6, 12, 14, 25)

Survival Guide

Prague Main Train Station (p147) PETR SVOBODA/SHUTTERSTOCK©

Before You Go

Book Your Stay

o Air-conditioning isn't necessary most of the year.

o Parking can be very tight. If driving, work out parking details with the hotel in advance and avoid hotels in Malá Strana and the Old Town.

o Many private singles or doubles in hostels are very nice and offer excellent value.

o You can often find last-minute bargains for top-end hotels on the standard online booking sites.

o Malá Strana is a particularly scenic location in which to stay, but it's worth considering a room in one of Prague's inner suburbs such as Vinohrady, Smíchov or Holešovice, as central Prague is easily reached by public transport.

Useful Websites

Alfa Tourist Service (☑ 224 230 037; www. alfatourist.cz; Opletalova

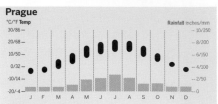

Prague

When to Go

o **Spring (Apr–Jun)** April is the start of tourist season. Accommodation is booked up at Easter and for the Prague Spring music festival in May.

o **Summer (Jul–Aug)** Sunny and occasionally hot. All attractions open.

o **Autumn (Sep–Oct)** Often sunny but cool. A handful of attractions close on 1 October for winter.

o **Winter (Nov–Mar)** Short, dark days, snow and blustery winds. Tourists descend for lively Christmas and New Year festivities.

38, Nové Město; ☺ 9am-5pm Mon-Fri; ☒ 5, 9, 15, 26) Can provide accommodation in student hostels, pensions, hotels and private rooms.

Mary's Travel & Tourist Service (☑ 222 253 511; www.marys. cz; Anny Letenské 17, Vinohrady; ☺ 9am-7pm Mon-Fri, 10am-5pm Sat & Sun; Ⓜ Jiřího z Poděbrad) Friendly, efficient travel agency specialising in finding accommodation in private rooms, hostels, pensions, apartments and hotels in all price ranges.

Navratilova Prague Apartments (☑ 604 168 756; www.prague-apart ment.com) Online service with comfortable, IKEA-furnished flats.

Lonely Planet (www. lonelyplanet.com) Author-recommended reviews and online booking.

Best Budget

o **Sir Toby's Hostel** (www.sirtobys.com) Dorms in a refurbished apartment building with a spacious kitchen and common room.

o **Sophie's Hostel** (www. sophieshostel.com) Hostel for a gentler sort of budget traveller, with a touch of contemporary style.

○ Ahoy! Hostel (www.ahoyhostel.com) Welcoming and peaceful hostel with eager-to-please staff and 'arty' decor.

○ Prague Central Camp (www.praguecentralcamp.com) Prague's most central campsite, located in Žižkov.

○ ArtHarmony (www.artharmony.cz) Central guesthouse with gimmicky decor.

Best Midrange

○ Domus Henrici (www.domus-henrici.cz) Peaceful seclusion a short stroll from the castle.

○ Mama Shelter Prague (www.parkhotel-praha.cz) Quirky design hotel in Holešovice.

○ Icon Hotel (www.iconhotel.eu) Very trendy designer hotel sporting 21st-century conveniences.

○ Hunger Wall Residence (www.hungerwall.eu) Spotlessly clean and modernised short-stay apartments.

○ Dům u velké boty (www.dumuvelkeboty.cz) Old pension set on a quiet square.

Best Top End

○ Golden Well Hotel (www.goldenwell.cz) Historic, luxury hotel in the ultimate location – beneath the castle walls.

○ Aria (www.ariahotel.net) Five-star luxury with a musical theme.

○ Dominican Hotel (www.dominicanhotel.cz) Housed in a former monastery, this hotel is bursting with character.

○ Alcron Hotel (www.alcronhotel.com) Central, five-star hotel with a Michelin-starred restaurant.

○ Le Palais Hotel (www.lepalaishotel.eu) Luxury hotel housed in a gorgeous belle-époque building.

Arriving in Prague

Václav Havel Airport Prague

This international **airport** (Prague Ruzyně International Airport; www.prg.aero; K letišti 6, Ruzyně; 🛜; 🚌100, 119) is 17km west of the city centre.

○ Airport Express (AE) Bus Runs between the airport and Prague's main train station at 30-minute intervals. Service starts at 5am and the last bus leaves around 9.30pm. Buy 60Kč tickets from the driver.

○ Fix Taxi (www.fix-taxi.cz) The official airport taxi company. A ride to náměstí Republiky costs about 600Kč.

○ Bus 119 This city bus terminates at the closest metro station to the airport, Nádraží Veleslavín (Line A). The whole trip to the centre is 32/16Kč per adult/concession. A luggage tickets costs an extra 16Kč.

Prague Main Train Station

Nearly all international trains arrive at Prague's main station, **Praha hlavní nádraží** (Prague Main Train Station; www.cd.cz; Wilsonova 8, Nové Město; Ⓜ Hlavní nádraží), connected to the rest of the city by metro Line C.

Note that some trains arrive at Prague's other large train station, **Praha-Holešovice** (Nádraží Holešovice; ☎840 112 113; www.cd.cz; Vrbenského,

Holešovice; MNádraží Holešovice), conveniently connected to the Nádraži Holešovice station on metro Line C.

Florenc Bus Station

Almost all international buses use **Florenc bus station** (ÚAN Praha Florenc; ☎221 895 555; www.florenc.cz; Pod výtopnou 13/10, Karlín; ⏱5am-midnight; 📶; MFlorenc), accessible by both the metro's B and C lines.

Getting Around

Prague has an excellent integrated public-transport system (www.dpp.cz) of metro lines, trams, buses

and night trams, but when you're moving around the compact Old Town or the castle area, it will be more convenient – and scenic – to use your feet. Times between tram stops are posted at each stop and on the website.

Metro

o The metro operates from 5am to midnight.

o There are three lines: Line A (green) runs from Nemocnice Motol in the west to Depo Hostivař in the east; Line B (yellow) runs from Zličín in the southwest to Černý Most in the northeast; and Line C (red) runs from Háje in the southeast to Letňany in the north.

o Services are fast and frequent. The nearest metro station is noted after the M in our listings.

o You must buy a ticket (jízdenka) before boarding, and then validate it by punching it in the little yellow machine in the metro-station lobby or on the bus or tram when you begin your journey. Checks by inspectors are frequent.

o You'll need coins for ticket machines at metro stations and major tram stops. You can also buy tickets at news stands, some hotels, tourist-information offices and metro-station ticket offices. Some machines can now handle contactless cards, but your foreign bank will charge you a hefty fee for the pleasure of paying this way.

Tram & Bus

o Important tram lines to remember are 22/23 (runs to Prague Castle, Malá Strana and Charles

Tickets & Passes

Tickets are interchangeable on all metros, trams and buses. Buy tickets at metro stations or nearby news stands – but never from the driver. If you're staying longer than a few hours, it's easier to buy a one-day or three-day pass.

Short-term ticket Valid for 30 minutes; adult/concession 24/12Kč

Basic ticket Valid for 1½ hours; adult/concession 32/16Kč

One-day ticket Valid for 24 hours; adult/concession 110/55Kč

Three-day ticket Valid for 72 hours; 310Kč for all ages

Bridge), 17 and 18 (run to the Jewish Quarter and Old Town Square) and 11 (runs to Žižkov and Vinohrady).

o Regular tram and bus services operate from 5am to midnight (see www.dpp.cz for maps and timetables). After this, night trams (91 to 99) and buses (901 to 915) take over.

o All night trams intersect at Lazarská in Nové Město.

o Be aware that few tram or bus stops sell tickets. So if you're using single tickets, buy several in the metro station or at news stands, then save a couple of unstamped ones for later and validate them upon boarding.

Taxi

o Prague's taxis are known for scams. If a driver won't switch on the meter, find another taxi.

o Look for the 'Taxi Fair Place' scheme, which provides authorised taxis in key tourist areas. Drivers can charge a maximum fare and must announce the estimated price in advance.

o Within the city centre,

trips should be around 150Kč to 200Kč. A trip to the suburbs should be no more than 450Kč, and to the airport around 600Kč to 700Kč.

The following radio-taxi services are reliable and honest:

AAA Radio Taxi
(222 333 222; www. aaataxi.cz)

ProfiTaxi (14015; www.profitaxi.cz)

Essential Information

Accessible Travel

Prague and Czechia are behind the curve when it comes to catering to travellers with disabilities. One exception is the Prague Public Transport Authority, which is making all stations wheelchair-friendly. See www.dpp. cz for details.

o **Prague Wheelchair Users Organisation**

(Pražská organizace vozíčkářů; Map p68, F3; 224 826 078; www. presbariery.cz; Benediktská 6; 9am-4pm Mon-Thu, to 3pm Fri; M Náměstí Republiky) Works to promote

barrier-free architecture and improve the lives of people with disabilities. Consult the website for online resources.

o **Czech Blind United**

(Sjednocená Organizace Nevidomých a Slabozrakých v ČR; Map p112, F2; 221 462 462; www. sons.cz; Krakovská 21, Nové Město; 9am-noon & 2-4.30pm Mon; M Muzeum) Represents the vision-impaired; provides information but no services.

Business Hours

Banks 8am to 4.30pm Monday to Friday

Bars 11am to midnight or later

Main post office 2am to midnight

Shops 8.30am to 8pm Monday to Friday, to 6pm Saturday and Sunday

Restaurants 10am to 11pm, though kitchens often close by 10pm

Discount Cards

o If you intend to visit several museums during your stay, consider purchasing a Prague Card (www.praguecard.com), which offers free or discounted entry to around

50 sights. Included are Prague Castle, the Old Town Hall, the National Gallery museums, the Jewish Museum, the Petřín Lookout Tower and Vyšehrad.

○ The pass is available for two to four days, starting at 1550/1150Kč per adult/child for two days.

○ Cards can be purchased at various museums, private tourist centres and shops. They can also be purchased online through the card website.

○ Prague Card pass holders are no longer entitled to free travel on the city's public transport system.

Electricity

Type C
220V/50Hz

Type E
220V/50Hz

Emergencies

To dial a number in Prague from outside the country, dial your international access code, the Czechia country code, then the unique nine-digit number.

Czechia country code 📞	420
International access code 📞	00
Ambulance 📞	155
Fire 📞	150
Police 📞	112

LGBTIQ+ Travellers

Prague is a relatively tolerant destination for gay and lesbian travellers. Homosexuality is legal in Czechia, and since 2006 the country has allowed gay couples to form registered partnerships. The city has a lively gay scene, anchored mainly in Vinohrady, and is home to Europe's biggest annual gay pride march (www.praguepride.cz), held in August.

Travel Gay Europe (www.travelgay.com) Useful website with information on both Prague and Brno.

Prague Saints (www.praguesaints.cz) This recommended gay bar maintains a useful website on what's on in Prague.

Money

○ Credit cards are widely accepted.

○ The Czech crown (Koruna česká, or Kč) is divided into 100 hellers (h), though these tiny coins no longer circulate. Prices are sometimes denominated in fractions of crowns. In these instances, the total is rounded to the nearest whole crown.

○ Keep small change handy for public toilets and tram-ticket machines.

Money-Saving Tips

o Forget taxis – take a shuttle bus from the airport to the city, then walk or use public transport.

o Skip the sushi and eat Czech food; you'll find the best value for your crowns in pubs. Look for set-lunch specials.

o Local beer is much cheaper than wine (and delicious).

o Don't exchange cash at the airport. Instead, withdraw local currency with your ATM card.

o Don't worry about missing museums if cash is tight – Prague is best explored outdoors and on foot.

o When going to the theatre, you can get cheaper tickets for around 200Kč.

Tipping

The general advice on tipping is to round up the bill in restaurants, bars and taxis to the nearest 50Kč or 100Kč. This is what Czechs do.

Public Holidays

Banks, offices, department stores and some shops will be closed on public holidays. Restaurants, museums and tourist attractions tend to stay open.

New Year's Day 1 January

Easter Monday March/ April

Labour Day 1 May

Liberation Day 8 May

Sts Cyril & Methodius Day 5 July

Jan Hus Day 6 July

Czech Statehood Day 28 September

Republic Day 28 October

Struggle for Freedom & Democracy Day 17 November

Christmas Eve (Generous Day) 24 December

Christmas Day 25 December

St Stephen's Day 26 December

Safe Travel

Prague is a low-crime city and safer than most Western cities. Pickpocketing and petty theft, however, remain rife, especially around the main tourist attractions. If you are the victim of a pickpocket, report the crime as soon as possible at any nearby police station. Remember to retain any paperwork you might need for insurance purposes.

For lost or stolen passports, embassies can normally issue travel documents swiftly.

Toilets

Public toilets are only free in museums, galleries, concert halls, restaurants, shopping malls and on trains. Everywhere else you have to pay – this includes in train, bus and metro stations. Public toilets are normally staffed by attendants who charge from 10Kč upwards to use the facilities, though some automated systems

Dos & Don'ts

Greetings It's customary to say *dobrý den* (good day) when entering a shop, cafe or pub, and to say *na shledanou* (goodbye) when you leave. When meeting people for the first time, a firm handshake, for both men and women, is the norm.

Visiting If you're invited to someone's home, bring flowers or some other small gift for your host, and remove your shoes when you enter the house.

Manners On trams and metros, it's good manners to give up a seat to an elderly or infirm passenger.

have begun to make an appearance. Men's are marked *muži* or *páni,* and women's *ženy* or *dámy*.

Tourist Information

Prague City Tourism (www.prague.eu) offices are good sources of maps and general information, as well as an excellent resource for finding what's on. The website is in English.

Prague City Tourism – Airport (☑ 221 714 714; www.prague.eu; Terminals 1 & 2, Václav Havel Airport Prague, Ruzyně; ⊗ 8am-8pm; ☒ 100, 119)

Prague City Tourism – Rytířská (Map p84, D3; ☑ 221 714 714; www. prague.eu; Rytířská 12; ⊗ 9am-7pm; Ⓜ Můstek)

Prague City Tourism – Old Town Hall

(Map p84, C2; ☑ 221 714 714; www.prague.eu; Staroměstské náměstí 1, Old Town Hall; ⊗ 9am-7pm; Ⓜ Staroměstská)

Prague City Tourism – Wenceslas Square

(☑ 221 714 714; www. prague.eu; Václavské náměstí 42; ⊗ 10am-6pm; Ⓜ Můstek, Muzeum)

Visas

Generally not needed for stays of up to 90 days.

Responsible Travel

Overtourism

o Avoid controversial city-centre short-term rentals which have turned the some of

historical core into a ghost-town.

o Try not to frequent souvenir shops selling Russian matryoshka dolls, Hitler mugs, cannabis sweets and the like. Prague council have evicted these places from city properties but many still prosper.

Leave a Light Footprint

Prague has one of the world's best public transport systems – so use it! Ride sharing apps such as Uber contribute to Prague's congestion and are threatening the livelihoods of local taxi drivers.

Language

Czech belongs to the western branch of the Slavic language family. Many travellers flinch when they see written Czech, but pronouncing it is not as hard as it may seem at first. Most of the sounds in Czech are also found in English, and of the few that aren't, only one can be a little tricky to master – *rzh* (written as *ř*). Also, Czech letters always have the same pronunciation, so you'll become familiar with their pronunciation really quickly.

With a little practice and reading our pronunciation guides as if they were English, you'll be understood. Just make sure you always stress the first syllable of a word – in italics in this chapter – and pronounce any vowel written with an accent mark over it as a long sound. In this chapter (m/f) indicates masculine and feminine forms.

To enhance your trip with a phrasebook, visit lonelyplanet.com. Lonely Planet iPhone phrasebooks are available through the Apple App store.

Basics

Hello.
Ahoj.   uh·hoy

Goodbye.
Na shledanou.   nuh·skhle·duh·noh

Excuse me.
Promiňte.   pro·min'·te

Sorry.
Promiňte.   pro·min'·te

Please.
Prosím.   pro·seem

Thank you.
Děkuji.   dye·ku·yi

Yes./No.
Ano./Ne.   uh·no/ne

Do you speak English?
Mluvíte   mlu·vee·te
anglicky?   uhn·glits·ki

I don't understand.
Nerozumím.   ne·ro·zu·meem

Eating & Drinking

I'm a vegetarian. (m/f)
Jsem   ysem
vegetarián/   ve·ge·tuh·ri·an/
vegetariánka.   ve·ge·tuh·ri·an·ka

Cheers!
Na zdraví.   nuh *zdruh*·vee

That was delicious!
To bylo lahodné!   to bi·lo *luh*·hod·nair

Please bring the bill.
Prosím   pro·seem
přineste   przhi·nes·te
účet.   oo·chet

I'd like ... , please. (m/f)
Chtěl/Chtěla   khtyel/khtye·luh
bych ..., prosím.   bikh ... pro·seem

a table	*stůl*	stool
for (two)	*pro (dva)*	pro (dvuh)
that dish	*ten pokrm*	ten
	po·krm	
the drinks	*nápojový*	na·po·yo·vee
list	*lístek*	lees·tek

Shopping

I'm looking for ...
Hledám ...   hle·dam ...

How much is it?
Kolik to stojí?   ko·lik to sto·yee

That's too expensive.
To je moc drahé.   to ye mots druh·hair

Can you lower the price?
Můžete mi   moo·zhe·te mi
snížit cenu?   snyee·zhit tse·nu

Emergencies

Help!
Pomoc!   po·mots

Call a doctor!
Zavolejte   zuh·vo·ley·te
lékaře!   lair·kuh·rzhe

Call the police!
Zavolejte   zuh·vo·ley·te
policii!   po·li·tsi·yi

I'm lost. (m/f)
Zabloudil/   zuh·bloh·dyil/
Zabloudila   zuh·bloh·dyi·luh
jsem.   ysem

I'm ill. (m/f)
Jsem nemocný/   ysem ne·mots·nee/
nemocná.   ne·mots·na

Where are the toilets?
Kde jsou toalety?   gde ysoh to·uh·le·ti

Time & Numbers

What time is it?
Kolik je hodin?   ko·lik ye ho·dyin

It's (10) o'clock.
Je jedna   ye yed·nuh
hodina.   ho·dyi·nuh

At what time?
V kolik hodin?   f ko·lik ho·dyin

morning	ráno	ra·no
afternoon	odpoledne	ot·po·led·ne
evening	večer	ve·cher

yesterday	včera	fche·ruh
today	dnes	dnes
tomorrow	zítra	zee·truh
1	jeden	ye·den
2	dva	dvuh
3	tři	trzhi
4	čtyři	chti·rzhi
5	pět	pyet
6	šest	shest
7	sedm	se·dm
8	osm	o·sm
9	devět	de·vyet
10	deset	de·set

Transport & Directions

Where's the ...?
Kde je ...?   gde ye ...

What's the address?
Jaká je   yuh·ka ye
adresa?   uh·dre·suh

Can you show me (on the map)?
Můžete   moo·zhe·te
mi to ukázat   mi to u·ka·zuht
(na mapě)?   (nuh muh·pye)

A ticket to ..., please.
Jízdenku   yeez·den·ku
do ..., prosím.   do ... pro·seem

What time does the bus/train leave?
V kolik hodin   f ko·lik ho·dyin
odjíždí   od·yeezh·dyee
autobus/vlak?   ow·to·bus/vluhk

I'd like a taxi.
Potřebuji   po·trzhe·bu·yi
taxíka.   tuhk·see·kuh

Is this taxi available?
Je tento taxík   ye ten·to tuhk·seek
volný?   vol·nee

Behind the Scenes

Send Us Your Feedback

We love to hear from travellers – your comments help make our books better. We read every word, and we guarantee that your feedback goes straight to the authors. Visit **lonelyplanet.com/contact** to submit your updates and suggestions.

Note: We may edit, reproduce and incorporate your comments in Lonely Planet products such as guidebooks, websites and digital products, so let us know if you don't want your comments reproduced or your name acknowledged. For a copy of our privacy policy visit lonelyplanet.com/privacy.

Marc's Thanks

Huge thanks goes to fellow author Mark Baker for all his advice and tips, to Paddy Tucker of Vinohrady, Ondra Krátký and my wife Tanya for all her support.

Mark's Thanks

I would like to thank my editors at Lonely Planet, my co-authors Marc Di Duca and Barbara Woolsey, and lots of people in my adopted home country of Czechia. These include Kateřina Pavlitová at prague.eu, Zuzi and Jan Valenta at tasteofprague. com, Magdaléna Soukupová in Plze.

Barbara's Thanks

A big thanks to all those who have helped me in this research and along the way: Clair Woolsey, Remy Woolsey, René Frank, Tiggy, Marlene Dow and family, Ardelle and George Kuchinka, Jean Cepe, Rose Caluza, Garth and Gloria Pickard, Richard Marcotte, Nolan Janssen, Ila Wenaus, and Jackie Tri.

Acknowledgements

Cover photograph: Strahov Monastery, Hradčany, Luigi Vaccarella/4Corners Images ©

This Book

This 6th edition of Lonely Planet's *Pocket Prague* guidebook was researched and written by Marc Di Duca, Mark Baker and Barbara Woolsey. The previous edition was written by Marc Di Duca, Mark Baker and Neil Wilson. This guidebook was produced by the following:

Senior Product Editor
Daniel Bolger

Regional Senior Cartographer Valentina Krementchutskaya, Julie Sheridan

Product Editors Kate Chapman, Martine Power, Saralinda Turner

Book Designer Michael Weldon, Hannah Blackie

Assisting Editors Andrew Bain, Victoria Harrison, Amy Lynch, Mani Ramaswamy, Rachel Rawling, Angela Tinson

Cover Researcher
Naomi Parker

Thanks to Fergal Condon, Joel Cotterell, Karen Henderson, Darren O'Connell, Genna Patterson

Index

See also separate subindexes for:

⊗ **Eating p158**
◉ **Drinking p159**
✪ **Entertainment p159**
◉ **Shopping p159**

Our Writers

Marc Di Duca

A travel author for over a decade, Marc has worked for Lonely Planet in Siberia, Slovakia, Bavaria, England, Ukraine, Austria, Poland, Croatia, Portugal, Madeira and on the Trans-Siberian Railway, as well as writing and updating many guides for other publishers. When not on the road, Marc lives near Mariánské Lázně in the Czech Republic with his wife and two sons.

Mark Baker

Mark Baker is a freelance travel writer with a penchant for offbeat stories and forgotten places. He's originally from the United States, but now makes his home in the Czech capital, Prague. He writes mainly on Eastern and Central Europe for Lonely Planet, as well as other leading travel publishers, but finds real satisfaction in digging up stories in places that are too remote or quirky for the guides.

Barbara Woolsey

Barbara Woolsey was born and raised on the Canadian prairies to a Filipino mother and Irish-Scottish father – and that multicultural upbringing has fuelled a life's passion for storytelling across cultures and borders. She's voyaged across five continents and almost 50 countries by plane, train and motorbike. In addition to writing for Lonely Planet, Barbara contributes to newspapers, magazines, and websites around the world. She spends most of her time in her adopted home of Berlin, Germany

Published by Lonely Planet Global Limited
CRN 554153
6th edition – February 2022
ISBN 978 1 78701 750 4
© Lonely Planet 2021 Photographs © as indicated 2022
10 9 8 7 6 5 4 3 2 1
Printed in Singapore